HOLLYWOOD COLLECTIBLES

Dian Zillner

Photographs by Suzanne Silverthorn
Consultant Editor Jeff Zillner

Value Guide included

Featuring Collectibles
From 20 Different Stars
Including Shirley Temple
and the Dionne Quints

Schiffer Publishing Ltd

1469 Morstein Road, West Chester, Pennsylvania 19380

Dedicated to Flossie Scofield, my mother, who escorted a reluctant ten-year-old child to a Saturday matinee which began my life-long fascination with the movies and their stars.

Value guide included

Copyright © 1991 by Dian Zillner.
Library of Congress Catalog Number: 90-64232.

Photographs by Suzanne Silverthorn
Consultant Editor Jeff Zillner
Printed in the United States of America.
ISBN: 0-88740-304-2

We are interested in hearing from authors with book ideas on related topics.

Published by Schiffer Publishing, Ltd.
1469 Morstein Road
West Chester, Pennsylvania 19380
Please write for a free catalog.
This book may be purchased from the publisher.
Please include $2.00 postage.
Try your bookstore first.

CHARLIE'S BACK!

Contents

Introduction

I fell in love with the movies when I saw my first film at the age of ten. For the next several years, all my weekly allowance was divided between the purchase of movie magazines and admission tickets at the neighborhood theater. I spent hours compiling dozens of scrapbooks filled with pictures of my favorite Hollywood stars.

As an adult, after my children were grown, I again began to pursue my childhood hobby. This time I have been more selective in the material I've purchased and have concentrated on stars that I particularly admire.

When I began my current collection, I found it very difficult to know what kinds of items were available for individual stars and I had to learn about the field mostly by trial and error.

I hope this book will help educate other collectors so they will have a better idea of the products that were made so they will be able to search out favorite items in a more systematic manner. The many pictures in the book are intended to demonstrate to future collectors the diversity of items which are available.

At the end of the last chapter, a list of addresses is given to help collectors in their search for movie material. Also included is a bibliography of the many books used to research this volume of movie memorabilia. I hope it will provide helpful sources for those collectors who want to explore further the lives of their favorite stars.

A special "thank you" goes to the members of my family who were so helpful during the writing of this book. To my son, Jeff Zillner who proved to be a very good consulting editor and my daughter, Suzanne Silverthorn, who did the photography, an extra special vote of appreciation.

I also want to express my thanks to the many collectors and writers who answered questions and shared material in order to make this book possible. Special acknowledgments go to: Marge Meisinger, Daryl Christensen, Judy Lawson, Blanche Trinajstick, Bartine Dickerson, Colleen Heidbreder, Mary and Ray Baker, Stan and Jim Shivers, Mark Silverthorn and Flossie Scofield. Perhaps the best part of being a collector is making new friends and being able to realize that there are still people who care.

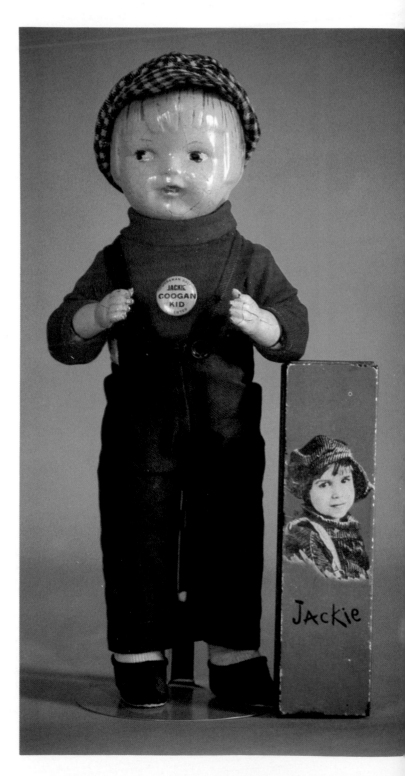

Fred Astaire

Dancer With Class

An autographed picture of Fred Astaire is a favorite collectible for Astaire fans.

Fred Astaire's career spanned seven decades. He was successful in all areas of entertainment including vaudeville, Broadway musicals, night clubs, radio, movies, and television. Some critics have called him the greatest American dancer ever. He certainly was the best in the history of the movies.

Astaire is remembered for both his dancing ability and because he was a well-liked gentleman. There aren't many men who can seriously be called a "gentleman," and no one had as much class as Fred Astaire.

Surprisingly, the debonair Astaire was born a midwesterner in Omaha, Nebraska in 1899 with the real name of Frederick Austerlitz. The family also included sister Adele, who was one year older. Because Adele seemed to be especially talented, she was given dancing lessons and she thrived on the experience. She became so good her parents decided she should have a chance for a dancing career and Mrs. Austerlitz took the two children to New York where she enrolled them in the Claude Alvienne Academy.

Fred had not been especially interested in Adele's dancing, but at the age of five he was given the role of supporting player for his sister's dancing act. This role was to continue until Adele's retirement in 1931.

Mr. Austerlitz stayed home in Omaha in order to support the New York trio in their show business endeavor. The children made their professional debut in Keyport, New Jersey about a year later using the names of Adele and Fred Astaire. They received $50 for their first week of work. The dancers continued to find bookings in the smaller communities around New York City until they were hired for the Orpheum circuit. By then, they were making $150 per week. The children were successful vaudeville performers until Fred reached the age of ten. Although Adele was blossoming into an attractive young lady, Fred still looked like a child and could no longer continue as his sister's dancing partner. The family decided to take time off to give Fred time to grow and they settled down for two years of regular schooling and rest. At the end of the hiatus, the dance team had to begin all over with new material and new bookings. Again, the dancers worked their way up from the small towns to theaters in the cities and again they attained success. The brother and sister's last vaudeville tour was in the 1915-1916 season.

The team was offered an opportunity to move from the vaudeville circuit to a Broadway musical in 1917. Their first show was a review for Lee and J.J. Shubert called *Over the Top*. After several more shows in New York, the Astaires took a hit musical called *For Goodness Sake* to London where it was retitled *Stop Flirting* in 1923. The brother and sister were an even bigger hit in London and the duo began a routine of doing a show in New York until it closed and then taking it to London to play for several months. The Astaires became friends with royalty and socialized with the elite of Britain during their tours to England. The last Broadway show the dance team did together was *The Band Wagon* in 1931. Adele retired from show business after the close of this show to marry Charles Cavendish and became, herself, a part of the British aristocracy.

Although Fred and Adele Astaire had been successful in vaudeville, musical comedy, and a few night club engagements, most of the critical acclaim had been directed toward Adele with Fred only praised as her partner. When Adele retired, Fred was under tremendous pressure to see if he could be a success as a single. He made one more appearance in a Broadway show called *The Gay Divorce* in 1932. Although the show was a moderate success, Fred decided to try Hollywood and the movies after so many years on the stage. He got in touch with Leland Hayward who talked to David Selznik, head of RKO at that time. Hayward got Astaire a contract with RKO to play in a musical film called *Flying Down to Rio*.

This original program for the Broadway hit musical *The Bandwagon* starring Fred and Adele Astaire dates from 1931.

An ad for the first Fred Astaire and Ginger Rogers film appeared in *Movie Mirror* for January, 1934. The 1933 RKO picture was called *Flying Down to Rio*.

Fred had been courting an Eastern socialite named Phyllis Potter for some time and they were married on July 12, 1933 before Fred was due in Hollywood to begin his movie career. Phyllis had a four year old son, Peter, from a previous marriage.

When the newly married couple arrived in Hollywood, Fred found that he was to be loaned to Metro-Goldwyn-Mayer to make a guest appearance in a film called *Dancing Lady* before his career would begin at RKO. The stars of the first Astaire film were Clark Gable and Joan Crawford. Fred did one dance with Crawford and he was able to play himself, even using his own name.

The stars of Fred's new RKO movie were Dolores Del Rio and Gene Raymond. Ginger Rogers was selected as Fred's dancing partner in the film. He and Ginger had known each other in New York during their Broadway days and had even had a few dates at that time. Fred and Ginger did a dance sequence in their new film called "The Carioca" and it proved to be a sensation. The new team stole the picture from the leading players and became an instant hit. RKO paired Rogers and Astaire for eight more movies before the partnership was dissolved: *The Gay Divorcee* 1934; *Roberta* 1935; *Top Hat* 1935; *Follow the Fleet* 1936; *Swing Time* 1936; *Shall We Dance* 1937; *Carefree* 1938; and *The Story of Vernon and Irene Castle* 1939. *Top Hat* and *Swing Time* are generally considered to be the best of the films but all of them are enjoyable. The public loved the new dance team and by 1935 the duo was listed in fourth place among the top box office stars of the country.

One of the great numbers in the 1934 RKO movie *The Gay Divorcee* was danced to "The Continental." The song was by Con Conrad and Herbert Magidson. This was the second Astaire—Rogers movie. The music was published by Harms.

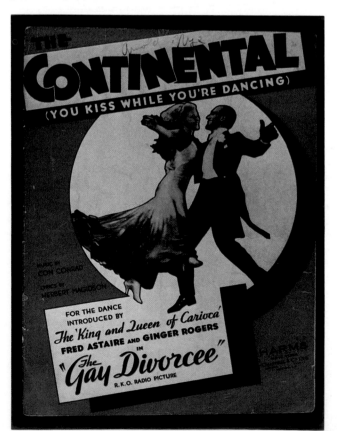

RKO's *Roberta* from 1935 had Astaire and Rogers sharing the starring roles in the picture with Irene Dunn and Randolph Scott. The song "Yesterday" was by Jerome Kern and Otto Harbach. It was published by T. B. Harms and was copyrighted by Jerome Kern.

One of the best of the RKO Astaire Rogers movies was *Top Hat* made in 1935. Irving Berlin supplied the music including this classic "Cheek to Cheek". The song was published by Irving Berlin, Inc.

"I'm Putting All My Eggs in One Basket" is a song from the Rogers-Astaire hit RKO picture *Follow the Fleet* from 1936. The music for the film was by Irving Berlin and it was published by Irving Berlin, Inc.

This sheet music is from the 1936 RKO Radio Picture *Swing Time* starring Fred Astaire and Ginger Rogers. The song is "A Fine Romance" by Jerome Kern and Dorothy Fields. It was published by Chappell and Co. and was copyrighted by Jerome Kern.

Pictured is a song book from the RKO Astaire—Rogers film from 1937 called *Shall We Dance*. All the George and Ira Gershwin songs from the movie are included in the book. It was published by Chappell and Co. and was copyrighted by Gershwin Pub. Co.

The 1938 RKO Rogers—Astaire musical was *Carefree* with music by Irving Berlin. Sheet music for "Change Partners" is pictured here. It was published by Irving Berlin, Inc.

Today's fans still appreciate the movie memorabilia of the most famous dance team in cinema history but the lobby cards and movie posters from these early films are prohibitive in cost for most collectors. The sheet music from the films is still reasonably priced and items like the *Life* magazine for August 22, 1938 with Rogers and Astaire on the cover are also affordable. One of the most prized mementos of the Astaire-Rogers films is a photograph autographed by the two stars. This is one collectible that will always be highly valued.

Ginger Rogers wanted to make films in addition to the musicals she was doing with Astaire and she continued to also make dramatic films throughout the 1930s. Fred, too, decided to try another film for RKO on his own in 1937. It was called *Damsel in Distress* with George Burns and Gracie Allen. It was not a successful picture at the time, though the famous hit song, "Foggy Day" did come from the dismal movie. It has been said that song writers loved to have Astaire sing their music in movies. Even though his voice was not trained, he had a way with lyrics and introduced many hits including: "The Way You Look Tonight", "Night and Day" and "Cheek to Cheek."

Besides having a successful movie career, Astaire was also experiencing a happy family life. His son, Fred Jr. was born in 1936 and a daughter Ava joined the family in 1942. Astaire also took an interest in horses and owned several race horses. One, named Triplicate, earned $250,000 in winning races.

After the last Astaire-Rogers film in 1939, Fred had to find another dancing partner. Through the years, he danced with a number of different co-stars. Many of them were far better dancers than Ginger Rogers but the chemistry was never quite as good as it had been between Fred and Ginger. The two stars still remain America's favorite dance duo.

One of Fred's partners was Paulette Goddard who starred with him in another forgotten picture he made for Paramount called *Second Chorus* in 1940. Fred must have felt badly to find himself making clinkers while Ginger was winning an Oscar for *Kitty*

One of the most prized collectibles for Astaire collectors is an autographed photo signed by both Astaire and his most famous partner, Ginger Rogers.

In 1937 RKO teamed Astaire with George Burns and Gracie Allen in *A Damsel in Distress*. A song from the picture, "A Foggy Day" by George and Ira Gershwin was a hit even if the picture wasn't. The music was published by Chappell and Co. and the copyright was by Gershwin Pub. Corp.

Astaire co-starred with fine tap dancers Eleanor Powell and George Murphy in *Broadway Melody of 1940* made for Metro-Goldwyn-Mayer. This postcard was used to promote the film.

Foyle in 1940. Another Astaire film for 1940 was made for M-G-M with co-star Eleanor Powell. It was called *Broadway Melody of 1940*. Although the picture did all right, it was not a hit and it was the last in the series of "Melody" movies. Fans today can enjoy the tap dancing duet of Astaire and Powell, probably one of the greatest ever put on film. The two danced to Cole Porter's "Begin the Beguine."

Astaire's fortune changed in the early 1940s when he had two hits with co-star Rita Hayworth in films made for Columbia. There was quite a lot of publicity for the films because of Miss Hayworth's fame as a "pin-up-girl" during World War II. The first movie was called *You'll Never Get Rich* in 1941 and the second picture was *You Were Never Lovelier* made in 1942.

Also in 1942, Astaire made the first of two successful films for Paramount, with Bing Crosby. It was called *Holiday Inn* and the famous motel chain secured its name from this movie. The film has been replayed on television each year at Christmas and is still a favorite. Astaire and the other stars of the cast were immortalized in paper doll images as a commercial spin off of this movie. The paper dolls are called *Hollywood Personalities* and were published by Samuel Lowe in 1941.

The other movie with Bing Crosby was made in 1946 and was called *Blue Skies*. Although not as well remembered as other Astaire musicals, it was successful at the box office when it was released. A Decca 78 RPM record album from this movie has Astaire singing the famous song, "Puttin' On the Ritz" by Irving Berlin.

This lobby card showing Fred Astaire is from the Paramount movie *Second Chorus* from 1940. Paulette Goddard was the co-star.

You Were Never Lovelier the Columbia film starring Astaire with lovely Rita Hayworth was made in 1942. Decca Records produced a record album with Fred singing the songs from the film. The music was by Jerome Kern and Johnny Mercer. There were six different songs in the three record album. Additional Astaire Decca records included the album, *Holiday Inn*, "Dream Dancing, "I Can't Tell a Lie" and "Since I Kissed My Baby Goodbye".

This record album was produced by Decca Records in 1946 featuring music from the Paramount movie *Blue Skies* starring Astaire and Bing Crosby. Irving Berlin was responsible for the music. Five records were included in the album.

In 1943 Astaire was called back to RKO to make *The Sky's the Limit* with Joan Leslie. In this film Astaire, now past forty, found himself playing leading man to a seventeen-year-old. Perhaps this age difference contributed to the indifferent reviews the film received. Fred continued his career by returning to M-G-M in 1945 to star in the fantasy film, *Yolanda and the Thief.* The movie was not a box office success at the time but it has gained more followers in recent years. Astaire continued his career at M-G-M when he joined an all star cast in the 1946 film *Ziegfeld Follies.* Fred and the cinema's other great male dancing star, Gene Kelly, joined together for a duet in the movie.

Fred Astaire hung up his dancing shoes and decided to retire after making *Blue Skies* in 1946, but was persuaded to return to movies after Gene Kelly broke his ankle and could not star in the M-G-M Judy Garland musical, *Easter Parade* in 1948. This film became one of the all time great Astaire musicals. With this success Astaire forgot about retirement and continued to choreograph new dance routines. When Judy Garland was unable to play the role, he was reunited with Ginger Rogers for *The Barkleys of Broadway* 1949 M-G-M picture. Ten years had passed since the two had last made a film together. Although they were both still great stars, the old chemistry was gone and the film was not up to the standards of their pictures from the 1930s. The 1950 M-G-M film called *Three Little Words* with Red Skelton and Astaire playing Harry Ruby and Bert Kalmar was another success for Astaire.

Also in 1950, he made *Let's Dance* for Paramount with co-star Betty Hutton. It was not successful, but in 1951 Fred had another hit at M-G-M with *Royal Wedding* (with Jane Powell who replaced a pregnant June Allyson). His next film for M-G-M was a loser called *Belle of New York* which he made with Vera-Ellen in 1952.

An unusual set of paper dolls was published by the Samuel Lowe Co. in 1941. The book was called *Hollywood Personalities* (#L1049) and featured the stars of the Paramount picture, *Holiday Inn.* Paper dolls of Fred Astaire, Bing Crosby, Marjorie Reynolds and Virginia Dale were in the set along with several chorus girls.

The Sky's the Limit co-starred Astaire with a very young Joan Leslie in 1943. The picture, made for RKO, was advertised in *Photoplay* magazine for September, 1943.

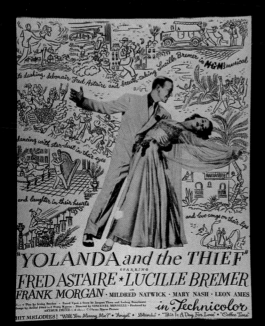

Fred Astaire joined an all-star cast in M-G-M's *Ziegfeld Follies* in 1946. The song is "Love" by Ralph Blane and Hugh Martin. Leo Feist, Inc. published the music.

This still from M-G-M's *Easter Parade* (1948) pictures stars Astaire and
Judy Garland. Irving Berlin provided the great songs.

An ad for the picture, *The Barkleys of Broadway*, a re-teaming of the
famous Astaire—Rogers dance team by M-G-M in 1949 did not re-
establish the duo as a desirable film couple. Although the film was
relatively successful, it was not the blockbuster their previous movies had
been.

M-G-M produced *Three Little Words* in 1950 with Fred Astaire and Red
Skelton playing the parts of song writers, Bert Kalmar and Harry Ruby.
"Thinking of You" was one of the hits by the famous team. Harm, Inc.
published the music.

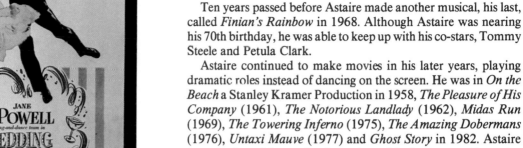

Astaire starred in many musicals throughout the 1950s with *The Bandwagon* (made for M-G-M with Cyd Charisse in 1953) considered to be one of his best. The hits continued with *Daddy Long Legs* co-starring Leslie Caron made for 20th Century-Fox in 1955 and *Funny Face* (Paramount) made in 1957 with Audrey Hepburn.

Astaire's last great M G M musical was produced in 1957 with Cyd Charisse. The movie was called *Silk Stockings* and was based on the 1939 Greta Garbo film, *Ninotchka*.

Ten years passed before Astaire made another musical, his last, called *Finian's Rainbow* in 1968. Although Astaire was nearing his 70th birthday, he was able to keep up with his co-stars, Tommy Steele and Petula Clark.

Astaire continued to make movies in his later years, playing dramatic roles instead of dancing on the screen. He was in *On the Beach* a Stanley Kramer Production in 1958, *The Pleasure of His Company* (1961), *The Notorious Landlady* (1962), *Midas Run* (1969), *The Towering Inferno* (1975), *The Amazing Dobermans* (1976), *Untaxi Mauve* (1977) and *Ghost Story* in 1982. Astaire was nominated for an Academy Award for best supporting actor for his part in *The Towering Inferno* in 1975. He was also seen in the films *That's Entertainment* and *That's Entertainment Part II* in the 1970s.

In addition to his success in movies, Fred Astaire also hosted a radio show in 1935. In it, he was a singing master of ceremonies for the *Lucky Strike Hit Parade*, as well as sometimes doing some dancing for the radio audience. Fred found that working in pictures and radio simultaneously was too hard and he gave up his radio program.

Movie Story for April, 1951 carried both the story and an ad for the M-G-M film *Royal Wedding*. The stars were Fred Astaire and Jane Powell.

The Band Wagon, made for M-G-M in 1953 is thought by some fans to be one of Astaire's best films. His co-star was Cyd Charisse. This still from the movie pictures Astaire, Nanette Fabray and Jack Buchanan.

A lobby card from one of the less successful Astaire films, *The Belle of New York* is pictured here. The M-G-M movie was made in 1952 with Vera-Ellen as co-star.

Astaire and Leslie Caron were new dancing partners in the 20th Century Fox film *Daddy Long Legs* in 1955. Johnny Mercer wrote the song "Something's Gotta Give" for the movie. Robbins Music Corp. published the music.

These paper dolls were based on the Warner Brothers film *Finian's Rainbow* from 1968 which starred Fred Astaire. The book was published by Saalfield in 1968 and is #1336.

With the closing of his dancing career in movie musicals, Fred began dancing on television. He did four television specials starting with a live show broadcast on NBC in October of 1958. He rehearsed for seven weeks with his partner, Barrie Chase, for the show called *An Evening With Fred Astaire*. The hard work paid off when Astaire earned his first Emmy.

Besides dancing on television, Astaire also acted in a dramatic series for the new medium. He co-starred with Robert Wagner in "It Takes a Thief" during the 1968-1969 seasons. The sixty-five episodes of the adventure spy thriller were later sold for syndication.

The Academy of Motion Picture Arts and Sciences also recognized Astaire's contribution to films when they awarded him an Academy Award in 1949 for his unique film artistry and for his contributions to the technique of musical pictures.

Astaire's wife Phyllis died of cancer in 1954 and Fred remained a bachelor for twenty-five years until he married Robyn Smith, a jockey, in 1980. His second wife proved to be a fine companion and the couple was very happy until Astaire's death in June, 1987 at the age of 88.

Pictured is the poster for the Astaire—Audrey Hepburn film *Funny Face* made for Paramount in 1957.

Fred Astaire was a perfectionist in his work. Whenever he entertained and through whatever medium he used, the audience was assured of high quality. His art, like his life, was delivered with elegance and class. Even though Astaire disliked his "uniform" of top hat, white tie, and tails, the image somehow seems appropriate for the man who came to embody graceful sophistication to all his admirers.

The World Doll Co. produced this vinyl doll representing Fred Astaire in 1987. The doll is wearing Astaire's well known "uniform" of top hat, white tie and tails. The doll is a portrait of Astaire as he looked in the M-G-M film, *The Barkley's of Broadway.* A companion Ginger Rogers doll was also made by the company in the same year.

James Cagney
Song and Dance Man

This studio picture of James Cagney was sent from William Cagney Productions for a short period in the mid-1940s when Cagney was making films for his family's company.

James Cagney thought of himself as a song and dance man, but most of his movie fans remember him as a tough guy with a humorous touch. The Cagney screen personality was cocky, charming, and full of energy. His staccato speech delivery was unique in the film industry. His only Academy Award, however, came from a song and dance movie, *Yankee Doodle Dandy* in 1942.

James Cagney was born in 1899 in the lower East Side of New York City. His father, James, was Irish and his mother, Carolyn, was Norwegian. Mr. Cagney was a charmer but he was not a very good provider for the family. He died when Jimmy was fourteen years old and before the youngest child of the family, Jeanne, was born. Jimmy and his three brothers all worked after school to supplement the family's income. Mrs. Cagney had a firm belief in the benefits of education, so all the children finished high school and went on to further education.

Jimmy Cagney grew up in a tough neighborhood. It made him a good street fighter, which came in handy later in his movie career when he played the parts of prize fighters.

The Cagneys were a close family and remained so all their lives. They all credited their mother for their good upbringing. While so many of their childhood friends ended up in prison, each of the Cagney children achieved success. Bill Cagney was Jimmy's business manager, Ed and Harry became doctors and Jeanne followed Cagney into the acting profession.

After Jimmy graduated from high school he attended Columbia University to study art. Unfortunately, money was short so he dropped out of school to find work to help the family with its finances. He heard of a job opening in the chorus of a Broadway show and someone suggested he try out. He only knew one dance, the "Peabody" he had learned in his neighborhood, but he was good at it and his interpretation of the dance got him the job. From then on, he improved his dance technique by watching what other dancers did and copying their steps. He danced so well he was hired for the show called *Pitter Patter* in 1920 and was given a specialty dance number in the production.

For the next few years he practiced his trade in vaudeville and stock shows. There he met his wife-to-be, Frances Vernon, and they were married in 1922. She, too, was a dancer and they formed a team and continued to work in vaudeville. In 1925 he appeared on Broadway in the play *Outside Looking In*. He continued to get occasional small parts in the Broadway shows to supplement his vaudeville work.

Cagney made his first real mark in the theater in *Maggie the Magnificent*, in 1929. Then came a show called *Penny Arcade* with Joan Blondell. Al Jolson saw the play and talked Warner Brothers into purchasing the story for a movie. Cagney and Blondell were signed to repeat their Broadway parts for the film. The movie, released in 1930, was called *Sinner's Holiday*.

Warners signed Cagney to a $400 per week contract, and put their new player to work at once. He made *Doorway to Hell* and the *Millionaire* with very little acclaim. Then came the film called *Public Enemy*. It was a story about two pals, one who is a quiet individual and the other who becomes a tough criminal. When the film was first cast, Cagney was to play the quiet boy while Eddie Woods was cast as the hoodlum. Bill Wellmen, the director, saw that they were miscast and was able to convince the head office to switch the parts. Cagney became the ruthless criminal that made him a star. The film was released in 1931 and went on to become a

Mae Clarke and Cagney are shown in the famous grapefruit scene from the Warner Brothers 1931 movie, *The Public Enemy*. Mae Clarke has autographed the print.

An advertisement for the Cagney—Humphrey Bogart movie, *Roaring Twenties* (Warners) appeared in *Screenland* magazine in November, 1939.

An ad for another popular Cagney film was featured in *Screen Book* magazine in September, 1939. The Warner film was *Each Dawn I Die* with another tough guy, George Raft, sharing starring honors with Cagney.

classic. Two of the scenes from the movie cannot be forgotten. The first, of course, is the famous grapefruit scene with Cagney and Mae Clarke when Cagney pushed half of a grapefruit into Mae's face during a breakfast squabble. The other memorable scene comes at the end of the picture when Cagney's family answers their front door and his corpse falls forward on its face into the room. This marvelous movie is available to fans on video cassette.

Cagney became known for his Warner Brothers crime pictures. He made several more through the 1930s with other Warner crime figures: Edward G. Robinson (*Smart Money*), Humphrey Bogart (*The Roaring Twenties*), and George Raft (*Each Dawn I Die*).

In 1933 Cagney was able to exchange his crime roles for a preferred dancing part in *Footlight Parade*. In the film, he played a producer of prologue stage productions to be shown at movie theaters before the film presentations. Busby Berkeley staged the dances in the picture and they were real extravaganzas. Ruby Keeler and Dick Powell provided the romantic element. The film grossed one and three-quarter million dollars.

In 1935, Cagney was one of many Hollywood stars who lent their talents to Warner's production of Shakespeare's *A Midsummer Night's Dream*. Although not characteristic of his screen roles, Cagney's reviews were good for his portrayal of Bottom but the film was not very successful.

Through the years Cagney had several conflicts with Warners over money. During 1935 and 1936 he worked for Grand National to make films because of a squabble with Warners. The pictures were not notable but after his hiatus he was able to return to the Warner studio with a contract to make five pictures at $150,000 each.

In 1936, the Cagneys purchased a farm in Martha's Vineyard and they spent as much of their leisure time there as possible. Jimmy's love of country living never left him. Cagney enjoyed the horses they raised and liked having the ocean close by so he could sail. It was a world away from Hollywood.

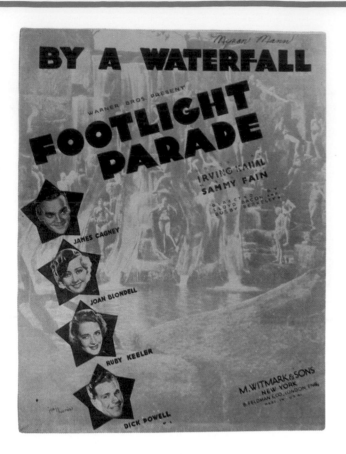

Pictured is sheet music from the 1933 Warner—Cagney musical hit, *Footlight Parade*. The song is "By a Waterfall" by Irving Kahal and Sammy Fain. It was published by M. Witmark and Sons in 1933.

Cagney lent his talents to Warners' all-star production of *Midsummer Night's Dream* in 1935. This ad appeared in *Screen Book* in November, 1935.

Back in Hollywood in 1936, Cagney teamed with Pat O'Brien in *Ceiling Zero*. O'Brien would be a frequent co-star and life-long friend. A book was based on this movie using photographs from the film to illustrate the story. The pair also starred in a less successful comedy for Warners called *Boy Meets Girl* in 1938.

A more successful 1938 Cagney-O'Brien film was the Warner crime picture called *Angels With Dirty Faces* with the "Dead End Kids." Ann Sheridan was the leading lady. The ending of the film is particularly interesting. The hood, Rocky (Cagney), is being sent to the electric chair to die. His friend from childhood (O'Brien), who has become a priest, comes to him and asks him to "turn yellow" as he is being led away so the kids who have an unhealthy admiration of him will have their hero's image destroyed. Rocky initially refuses the request but he does turn cowardly as he is being taken to die. Is it real? Is it an act? No one knows and the question is still to be answered.

Cagney's career continued to thrive. In 1935 he was listed in 10th place among the best of the Box Office Stars. In 1939 he was in ninth place and by 1940 he had reached fourth place. As the decade of the 1940s began, Cagney was in hit after hit film. He played a World War I soldier in *The Fighting 69th* with George Brent in 1940. In 1941 he made *Strawberry Blonde* with Olivia de Havilland and Rita Hayworth. It was a turn-of-the-century epic with just the right touch of humor and music. Another successful movie from the period was *Captains of the Clouds*, Cagney's first technicolor film made in 1942.

This *Ceiling Zero* book was based on the Warner movie with Pat O'Brien and James Cagney. It is illustrated with scenes from the film. The book was published by the Lynn Publishing Co. in 1936. Cagney movie items like this can still be purchased for $15 or under.

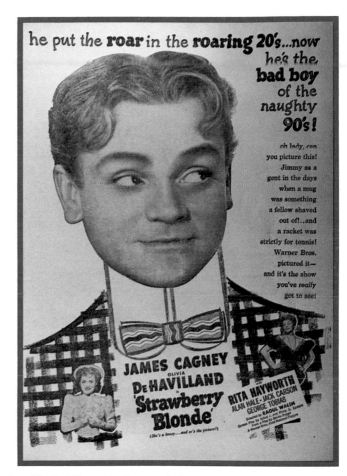

Cagney joined Pat O'Brien again in 1938 when they co-starred in the Warner comedy *Boy Meets Girl*. This ad was featured in *Movie Mirror* in August, 1938.

Standard Oil used this picture in 1940 to promote their gasoline as well as the new Warner Brothers movie, *The Fighting 69th*. In addition to Cagney, other stars featured in this give-away campaign were: Mary Martin, Ginger Rogers, Barbara Stanwyck, Cary Grant, Errol Flynn, Spencer Tracy and Ann Sheridan.

An ad for the Warner Brothers movie *Strawberry Blonde* starring Cagney, Olivia de Havilland, and Rita Hayworth. It appeared in the *Screen Romances* magazine in April, 1941.

During this same time, changes occurred in the Cagneys' personal lives as well. They adopted two children, Jim, Jr. and Cathleen and introduced them to the farm in the East. By this time, James Cagney was making the second highest salary of anyone in the United States. Louis B. Mayer, head of the M-G-M studios, was the only person paid more.

Then in 1942 came *Yankee Doodle Dandy*, Cagney's personal favorite among his movies. The story was based on the life of the great American song and dance man, George M. Cohan. The timing was perfect. World War II was in full swing and Cohan's patriotic songs were just right for the era. Cagney put on his dancing shoes and went into rehearsal to learn Cohan's stiff legged dancing style. The four Cohans were played by Walter Huston, Rosemary de Camp, Cagney and Jeanne Cagney. Jeanne, Cagney's sister, played the role of George Cohan's sister in the film. George M. Cohan, himself, was sick with cancer and he died later in 1942, but not before he was able to see the completed picture. James Cagney received the Academy Award for best actor of 1942 based on his performance in *Yankee Doodle Dandy*. The film took in over four million dollars.

Cagney joined his fellow actors during World War II giving performances for the USO and selling war bonds. He even made a trip to England to entertain the soldiers in 1944.

James Cagney broke up his long association with Warner Brothers after the completion of *Yankee Doodle Dandy* and he formed his own production company. He made the films, *Johnny Come Lately* in 1943, *Blood On the Sun* in 1944, and *The Time of Your Life* in 1948. None of these pictures were as popular as his earlier Warner films.

Perhaps Cagney realized this as he returned to Warners in 1949 to make his last big gangster picture, *White Heat*. It, too, has a memorable death scene for Cagney. At the end of the film, Cagney's character, Cody Jarrett, is trapped on the top of a huge gas tank and he is surrounded by police. Instead of giving himself up, he shouts, "Top of the world, Ma," shoots his gun into the tank, and blows himself and everything in the vicinity to kingdom come. Quite a spectacular ending even for a "bad guy." Cagney continued his "bad guy" character portrayal by teaming up with frequent co-stars, Ann Sheridan and Pat O'Brien, in the film *Torrid Zone* for Warners in 1950.

In 1950 Cagney returned to his true love, the musical, in *The West Point Story* with Doris Day. He was over fifty years old by that time, but, because he practiced his dancing regularly to keep in shape he was able to get back in the swing of things without too much difficulty. In 1951 Cagney again changed gears when he gave a fine performance in the film, *Come Fill the Cup*. He played an alcoholic trying to get his life back together and received very favorable reviews.

After making several films of questionable quality, Cagney appeared in two more hits in 1955. He played the unforgettable part of the captain in *Mr. Roberts* and the part of "The Gimp" Snyder in *Love Me or Leave Me*. "The Gimp" was the first husband of singer Ruth Etting and the film was the story of her life. Doris Day played Ruth.

One of the few magazines which featured James Cagney on its cover was this May, 1942 issue of *Screen Romances*. Joan Leslie shares the honors as they publicize their new film *Yankee Doodle Dandy*. An inside article also promoted the movie.

Sheet music from the Warners' 1942 movie *Yankee Doodle Dandy*. The music is by George M. Cohan and the songs shown are "Over There", "Yankee Doodle Boy" and "You're a Grand Old Flag". They were published by Jerry Vogel Music Co., Inc.

An advertisement for *Johnny Come Lately*, a film by the Cagney's own production company. The ad was in *Photoplay* magazine in October, 1943.

A window card from the movie *The West Point Story*, the Cagney starring vehicle produced by Warner Brothers in 1950.

This picture of James Cagney was given away by movie theaters to advertise the upcoming film *Torrid Zone* produced by Warner Brothers in 1950. Ann Sheridan and Pat O'Brien co-starred in the film.

A lobby card for the Cagney film *Come Fill the Cup*, a Warner Brothers film from 1951. Pictured are James Gleason and Cagney in a scene from the movie.

A scene from *Love Me Or Leave Me* is pictured on this lobby card. Shown are Doris Day as singing star Ruth Etting and Cagney as "The Gimp". The M-G-M film is from 1955.

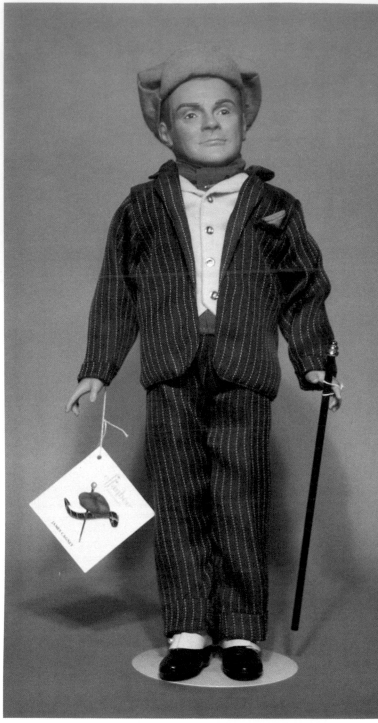

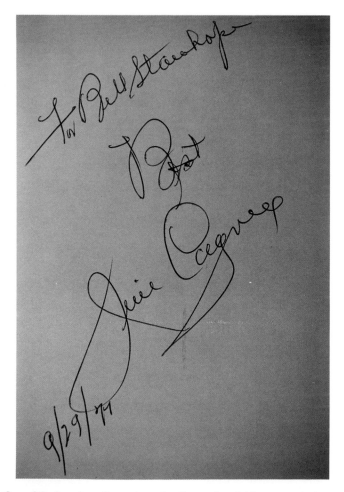

This vinyl James Cagney doll was made by the Effanbee Doll Co. in 1987 to honor the famous film star. He is dressed in the costume he wore in *Yankee Doodle Dandy* as he performed the Johnny Jones scene in the picture.

One of the favorite collector items for Cagney fans is his autograph, here shown on the inside page of his autobiography *Cagney by Cagney*, published by Doubleday and Co. in 1976.

These scenes are from James Cagney's last professional appearance. He played Joe Moran in a CBS ITT Theatre production of "Terrible Joe Moran," aired on March 27, 1984. Pictured with Cagney are Ellen Barkin and Art Carney who were also in the production.

Also in 1955, Cagney got out his dancing shoes once more to portray George M. Cohan in a cameo appearance in the Bob Hope movie, *The Seven Little Foys*, the story of Eddie Foy. Cagney, then fifty-six years old, had a bit more trouble preparing for the part, but after three weeks of rehearsal he was ready. The table top dance in the film is a delight and a favorite for Cagney fans.

In 1957 Cagney appeared in another film biography when he portrayed Lon Chaney in *Man of 1000 Faces*. He received good reviews for his acting, and continued the biography roles in 1960 when he played Admiral William F. Halsey in *The Gallant Hours*.

Cagney made what was supposed to be his last film appearance in 1961 in the Billy Wilder comedy called, *One, Two, Three* for United Artists. Then he retired to the New York farm he had purchased in 1955 to enjoy his horses, his family, and the countryside. He also reactivated his old interest in painting.

During his retirement, Cagney spent many hours working on his autobiography, *Cagney by Cagney*. The memories he shared in the book about his boyhood are especially interesting for today's readers. Fans particularly treasure copies of the book signed by Cagney, himself.

After refusing offers for film work for many years, Cagney agreed to play a cameo role in the picture *Ragtime* in 1981. The movie received lots of publicity because of his appearance and he seemed to enjoy the challenge. Cagney, however, quickly returned to the quiet of his farm after the filming was finished.

Cagney's last professional appearance was in a television production called *Terrible Joe Moran* in 1984. It was not all together successful. Cagney was too ill to really project the part and it was rather sad for his fans to see him try. But, of course, he had spunk until the last.

James Cagney died in 1986 at his farm in Dutchess county in New York with his wife of sixty-four years close by. He had been ill for some time with diabetes and circulatory problems.

"Gone but not forgotten", James Cagney's screen career is still highly regarded. The Effanbee Doll Co. created a doll in his memory in 1987. Fittingly enough, the doll is not dressed as a gangster but as a song and dance man from his movie role in *Yankee Doodle Dandy*. It is the way Cagney most wanted to be remembered.

Charlie Chaplin
The Little Tramp

The Charlie Chaplin Book was published by Sam'l Gabriel Sons and Co. circa 1915.

Charlie Chaplin's "Little Tramp" was probably the best known screen character in the world. With no language barrier in the silent film, people could enjoy the Chaplin humor no matter what language they spoke. This character has been immortalized not only in films but also through toys, comics, dolls, paper dolls, books, ashtrays and other knick-knacks. It has also been used in all sorts of commercial enterprises including recent television commercials.

Charles Chaplin was born in a poor district in London in 1889 where both of his parents were performers. His father, also Charles Chaplin, was a vocalist and his mother Lily Harley (her real name was Hannah) was a singer and dancer. The Chaplins did not stay together long and when Charlie's mother had to assume the support of herself and her two boys (Charlie's brother Sydney was a son from an earlier marriage), it was impossible for her to look after them. The family was separated when Charlie was still very young and he and Sydney spent two years in an orphanage beginning in 1894. Their mother had a nervous collapse and she spent many years in mental institutions. After Charlie's success, he brought her to California and she lived there until her death. When the boys were released from the orphanage they secured work wherever they could get it, doing all kinds of odd jobs.

With his stage background, it is not surprising that the young Chaplin leaned in that direction for his chosen career. By 1899 he was touring English music halls and in 1905 he had a part in the play *Painful Predicament of Sherlock Holmes*.

He then joined Fred Karno's Company and made two tours of the United States with it. The first trip was in 1910-1911 when he performed in *A Night in an English Music Hall*. During the second tour in 1912-1913, Chaplin was hired by Mack Sennett to do silent films and he went to Los Angeles to begin work in 1913.

Chaplin made his first film in 1914. It was a one-reeler called *Making a Living*. He was making $175 a week, much more money than he had ever made before. Apparently, Chaplin developed his tramp character quite by accident. In his second film, *Kid Auto Races in Venice*, he put together the tramp costume with borrowed pieces. Charlie Chaplin made thirty-five short films during his first year of film making.

In 1915 he changed to the Essanay Co. where he was paid $1,250 per week. Chaplin made fifteen films for Essanay before moving to the Mutual Film Corp. after they offered him $10,000 per week. In 1916, he made twelve movies for Mutual. In 1917 he once again changed direction when he began work for the First National Exhibitor's Circuit with the first million dollar contract in the movie industry. In 1918 he set up his own studio so he could make movies in his own way.

By this time Chaplin had achieved wide recognition and his tramp character was being used to promote various products. A wonderful child's book was published by Sam'l Gabriel Sons and Co. It featured many pictures of the Little Tramp. The book has been re-issued in the last few years as a reprint.

Toys were also being manufactured in the Chaplin image all through the years. A doll made in a very good likeness of the tramp character was produced by Louis Amberg and Son in 1915. It had a composition head, with painted features and molded hair. The hands were composition and the rest of the doll was cloth stuffed with straw. Usually a cloth label on the sleeve identified the doll as Charlie Chaplin.

Louis Amberg and Son produced this 14″ tall Charlie Chaplin doll in 1915. The doll has a composition head and hands with painted features and molded hair and a cloth body. His clothes are original and the jacket usually is marked with a label on the sleeve which reads: "Charlie Chaplin/World's Greatest Comedian/Made exclusively by Louis Amberg/and Son, N.Y./by special arrangement with/Essanay Film Co."

The *Charlie Chaplin Percy Reeves Movy-Dols* were published in 1919. The series also included several other silent stars including: Mary Pickford, Norma Talmadge, and May Allison.

Paper dolls, too, were made in the Chaplin form. Along with other silent stars, Chaplin was pictured in a set of paper dolls called *Percy Reeves Movy-Dols* in 1919. These paper dolls were also published in a book called *Percy Reeves Movy-Dols Painting Book #1*. This book contained paper dolls for the child to color. Besides Chaplin, movie stars included in the book are Mary Pickford, May Allison, and Norma Talmadge.

Chaplin's personal life (which would include many marriages during several decades) made headlines when Charlie married his first young wife in 1918. He was twenty-nine years old and his bride, Mildred Harris, was only sixteen. Even as Chaplin got older he continued to be romantically involved with very young women. The marriage to Miss Harris lasted only two years before they were divorced.

One of Chaplin's biggest hit films was *The Kid* with the child star Jackie Coogan made in 1920. Chaplin was his own writer, director, star, cutter, and composer of many of his films. This set him apart from other screen personalities of the day and led to many critics calling him a "film genius." *The Kid* grossed two and a half million dollars. The child star, Jackie Coogan, was also created as a doll wearing his costume from *The Kid*.

1920 was also the year that Chaplin joined three of the biggest names in the silent film industry to form the United Artists Company. Mary Pickford, Douglas Fairbanks, and D. W. Griffith, along with Chaplin, all wanted to be able to control their own pictures from inception to distribution and the new company enabled them to do just that.

Chaplin married for the second time in 1924 when he again chose a young bride, Lita Grey (real name Lolita McMurray). She was also only sixteen when they married. Two sons were born to the couple: Charles Jr. and Sydney. The marriage was stormy, as was the divorce in 1927.

Charlie was extremely popular with the public. His "Little Fella," as Chaplin himself called his character, was as busy as ever promoting products. A game called *Chasing Charlie* made by Spears Games of England and "Charlie" wooden boxes are two examples of Chaplin products. Germany was also intrigued with Charlie and a wind-up toy was manufactured there. A cartoon was drawn by J. Kelley and published in book form by M. A. Donohue and Co. in 1917. Even songs were written about Chaplin and his image. One called "Charlie Chaplin Walk" was published in 1915 and another called "At the Moving Picture Ball" was published in 1920. The latter song mentioned many of the silent film stars and pictured them on its cover. To capitalize on both the popularity of Charlie's fame and the fad of glass candy containers, a Charlie Chaplin figure was manufactured in this medium to add yet another product for collectors to add to Chaplin collections.

One of Chaplin's biggest hits, *The Gold Rush*, was released in 1925 to rave reviews. Some still think it is Chaplin's finest silent film. The pantomime of his cooking and eating one of his shoes when he was starving is truly great. The film had such staying power that it was released again in 1942 with a Chaplin musical score and some added sound effects. The movie can currently be seen via video cassette as can most of Chaplin's later films. The picture grossed two and a half million dollars during its original release.

Many decorative wooden boxes were produced with Chaplin's "Little Tramp" image on the covers and insides of the boxes. This handkerchief box is marked, "Charlie Chaplin © C.C.A.S. Co.".

This Jackie Coogan doll is dressed in his original clothes just as the real Jackie looked when he played in Chaplin's hit 1920 movie, *The Kid*. The doll was made by the E. I. Horsman Co. in 1921. He has a composition head and hands and a cloth body. The eyes are painted and his hair is molded. He is marked on the back of his neck "E. I. H. Co. 19 © 21." The doll is 14″ tall. Shown with the doll is a pencil box with Jackie's picture on the front. A similar box was also made in Charlie's image.

This 8″ tall metal wind-up Charlie Chaplin toy was manufactured in Germany circa 1920. He has cast iron feet and waddles along and rocks back and forth when wound. He has a blue coat, red tie and a cane. Photograph courtesy of Daryl and Mary Alice Christensen.

This large comic book called *Charlie Chaplin's Funny Stunts* was published by M. S. Donohue and Co. in 1917. The comic strips were drawn by J. Kelley in arrangement with Chaplin's studio at the time, Essanay Co.

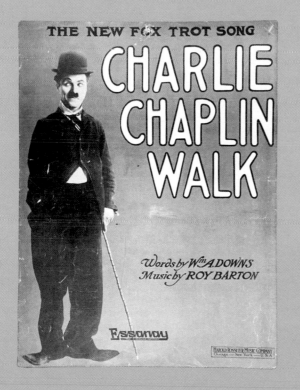

Pictured is sheet music called "Charlie Chaplin Walk" by Wm. A. Downs and Roy Barton. The Essanay name appears under Charlie's picture. The song was published in 1915 by the Harold Rossiter Music Co. Early sheet music of Chaplin is sought after by today's collectors.

The sheet music called "At the Moving Picture Ball" features Charlie Chaplin's photograph on its front cover and he is mentioned in the lyrics. The song is by Howard Johnson and Joseph Santly and it was published by Leo Feist, Inc. in 1920.

Capitalizing on the popularity of candy containers and the Chaplin image, this candy container was manufactured. It has a figure of Chaplin along with a barrel to hold the candy. The name "Charlie Chaplin" is printed in the glass under Charlie's feet. On the bottom of the container is: "Geo. Borgfeldt and Co. New York Sole Licensees Patent Applied For Serial No. 2862."

This Omaha, Nebraska newspaper for September 20, 1925 carried a large ad for Chaplin's new movie, *The Gold Rush*. The movie became quite a hit for Chaplin.

At about this same time, another product was put on the market in England to take advantage of the popular Chaplin image. Although the toy is only called "Dancing Charlie" there is no doubt it is intended to represent Charlie Chaplin. Chaplin was not forgotten by the American toy industry either. A game called *Movie-Land Keeno* was manufactured in 1929 by the Wilder Manufacturing Co. which featured Charlie's picture on the cover.

Because Chaplin did everything on his films, it took him several years to finish one movie. *The Circus* was released in 1928 but it was not a big hit like his other pictures had been. It was not until 1931 that Chaplin had his next successful film. Between the time of *The Circus* in 1928 and *City Lights* in 1931, the film industry had undergone major changes. Sound had been added to movies and silent pictures had been dropped by all the studios. The tramp character was so well known that Chaplin was afraid a voice might spoil his appeal so the new film was finished as it was begun; as a silent movie. *City Lights* is one of Chaplin's most sentimental films. The movie did surprisingly well at the box office. It grossed over one million dollars, was the fourth biggest money maker of the year, and was chosen as one of the ten best pictures of the year by the *The New York Times*.

Headlines over the Chaplin personal life were again in evidence during the mid 1930s. He had become involved with another young starlet, Paulette Goddard, and although they seemed to be living together they had never announced a marriage. Even in 1939 there were still questions regarding their private life when *Screen Book* magazine asked "Paulette Goddard-Why is she Called Hollywood's Mystery Woman?" referring to her still unannounced marriage to Chaplin. Eventually it was established that they were married in 1936 while working on the Chaplin film, *Modern Times* (they were divorced in 1942). Goddard was featured in the movie along with the Little Tramp. This was the last silent film for Chaplin and the last picture featuring his "Little Fella." Because of its subject matter, this movie has remained one that especially appeals to film goers today. The film was about the importance of the individual in the machine age and how men were just becoming cogs in the machinery. It pictured Chaplin as an assembly line worker doing the same repetitive task hour after hour. Since this movie was made during the depression, Chaplin also managed to criticize injustice to his fellow man in addition to making people laugh. The picture was a huge success grossing over $1,888,000 and was only beaten in earnings by the year's blockbuster film, *San Francisco*. With the ending of Chaplin's career as "The Little Tramp" the pictures sent out to fans from United Artists showed Chaplin as he looked in real life instead of in the more familiar role of the tramp.

Again several years elapsed before the next Chaplin movie was ready for the public. *The Great Dictator* came along in 1940. In the film, Chaplin played a dual role-that of a dictator based on Adolf Hitler and that of a Jewish barber. With the war raging in Europe, Chaplin was one of the first film makers to satirize Hitler and Mussolini. The film was Chaplin's first talkie. It grossed two million dollars and was the top money maker of 1941, with the film receiving so much publicity because of its Hitler connection. A set of paper dolls was produced to tie-in to the movie which featured Chaplin and Paulette Goddard who was also in the film. They were printed by Saalfield Publishing Co. in 1941. These paper dolls are among the most sought after by collectors so they may be expensive. Saalfield also produced a Charlie Chaplin coloring book during this same year.

Pictured is a "Dancing Charlie" cardboard toy produced in England around 1925. It is shown with the original envelope.

An advertisement from Chaplin's still silent film, *City Lights* from 1931. The picture was a coming attraction at Loew's Broadway Theater and was featured in their weekly publication for May 16, 1931.

This *Movie-Land Keeno* game by A. J. Saxe was manufactured by the Wilder Manufacturing Co. in 1929. Charlie Chaplin's picture is featured on the front cover along with several other popular Hollywood stars of the time.

Screen Book for September, 1939 was still examining the mystery of the Goddard-Chaplin relationship in the cover story "Paulette Goddard: Why Is She Called Hollywood's Mystery Woman?" Paulette was featured on the cover of the magazine.

Chaplin's hit film from 1940 was called *The Great Dictator*. This is a program from the film.

With Charlie's new image in the movie *The Great Dictator* in 1940, fans began receiving studio publicity photos of the real Chaplin instead of the "Little Tramp" character. This picture was mailed from United Artists to a fan in November, 1940.

The Great Dictator received lots of publicity in 1940, partly because its theme was so in keeping with the current world situation in Europe. Two magazines that did cover stories on the film are pictured here. *Look* magazine for September 24, 1940 featured Chaplin in his role as Adenoid Hynkel and *Friday* for October 11, 1940 showed Jack Oakie in costume for his part as Napolini in the same film.

Although Chaplin would make four more movies during his long career, his fans in the United States began to abandon him beginning in the mid 1940s. Chaplin's personal life became more sensational than his professional life and he was judged (unfairly in many cases) to be un-American on many counts. His troubles seemed to begin during World War II when he made speeches to encourage a second front in the war against Germany and he became known as a Russian sympathizer.

About this same time a young starlet named Joan Barry brought a paternity suit against him saying he had fathered her child. This brought about a trial on a violation of the Mann act but he was acquitted. Two trials on the Barry case were held, and although blood tests showed he could not have been the child's father, he was still found guilty and ordered to pay child support. Before the court case was finished in 1943 he made even more headlines when he married his fourth young bride, Oona O'Neill (daughter of playwright Eugene O'Neill) who was only eighteen years old while he was fifty-four.

Controversy continued as Chaplin came under the scrutiny of right wing conservatives and in 1952, while Chaplin was on his way to England, the United States cancelled his re-entry permit and he wasn't allowed to return to his home in California. His estrangement from his adopted country would last for the next twenty years.

Paper dolls of Charlie Chaplin and Paulette Goddard were published by Saalfield in 1941 to tie in with the film called *The Great Dictator* which starred both performers. It is #2356 and is one of the most collectible of the paper doll books from the 1940s.

This movie still pictures Chaplin and Martha Raye in a scene from *Monsieur Verdoux*. The picture was released by United Artists in 1947.

He and Oona settled in Switzerland where they raised their eight children in relative peace. Chaplin continued to make films. In 1947 he made *Monsieur Verdoux*, a comedy about murder, which was not very successful. *Limelight*, a story about an aging clown, released in 1952, was a hit in England but not in the United States. In 1957 he made *A King in New York* which wasn't even shown in the United States.

In 1966 *Life* magazine showed it had forgiven Chaplin when it did a cover story on the star as he was making his last film *A Countess From Hong Kong* with Marlon Brando and Sophia Loren. It didn't help. The movie was not well received.

The rift was finally healed between Chaplin and the United States in 1972 when he was invited to receive awards by the New York Film Society and the Academy of Motion Picture Arts and Sciences. Charlie Chaplin was eighty-three years old by that time and the trip and the emotional trauma it produced were hard on the veteran entertainer. *Life* magazine covered the events with a cover story in their April 21, 1972 edition. At about this same time, Bubbles Inc. manufactured a vinyl doll in the "Little Tramp" image. Although it is not as good a likeness as the earlier Amberg doll, it has become a collector's item.

The Chaplins returned to their home in Switzerland where Chaplin continued to live in poor health until his death on Christmas day in 1977. The praise he received in his obituaries was a reminder to the public that Chaplin was still considered one of the screen's greatest film makers.

Charlie Chaplin made more than eighty movies from 1914-1967 and in most of them he played a character wearing a small jacket, baggy pants, shoes that were too large and a derby hat that was too small. His tiny mustache and the ever present walking cane completed the costume. To movie fans, the character represented much more than just a tramp-he was "everyman" involved in the human struggle-down but not out, always an optimist-never giving up. Perhaps that is why the "Little Fella" has been able to continue to promote products. "The Tramp" still symbolizes the hope and comedy that Charlie Chaplin's character represented for people all over the world for so many years.

A vinyl doll was made in the image of Chaplin's "Little Tramp" in 1972, perhaps as a result of Chaplin's visit to the U. S. It was made by Bubbles, Inc. and has a vinyl head, hands and feet, molded hair and derby hat, and painted features. The costume was similar to that worn by Chaplin's famous movie character. The doll is 20″ tall and carries a cane.

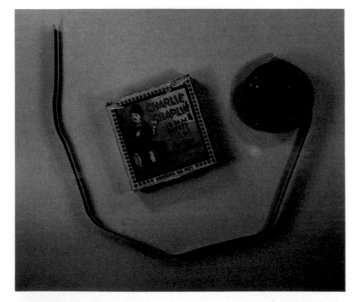

16 mm film of one of Chaplin's early movies called "Assistance Wanted" The product dates from the 1930s. The reel contains fifty feet of film and it was produced by Keystone.

Bing Crosby

The Top Entertainer

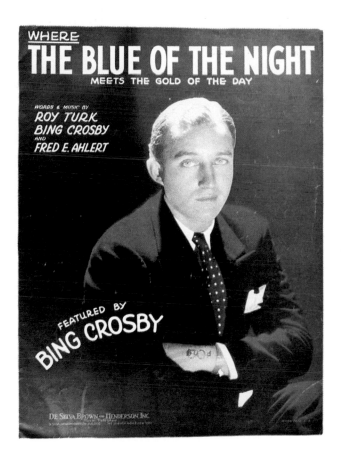

Sheet music for Bing Crosby's theme song, "Where the Blue of the Night Meets the Gold of the Day" which he helped Roy Turk and Fred Ahlert write. It was copyrighted and published by DeSylva, Brown and Henderson, Inc. in 1931, the year Bing Crosby's radio program began on CBS.

Many consider Bing Crosby the greatest entertainer of the 20th century. He was a star in radio, recording, television and, of course, movies. He was the number one box office star of motion pictures from 1944-1948 and is ranked as the second most popular star of sound pictures (after John Wayne). At his death, Bing was also the greatest selling recording artist of all time. These accomplishments plus the many years Bing Crosby worked in show business (fifty) give him a very good claim to the title of top entertainer of the 20th century.

Bing Crosby's public persona was that of an easy-going, relaxed, charming, fun-loving guy. Most of his fans thought the real Bing Crosby was like that as well. After his death it was reported that he was really more of a loner with few really close friends, a man who held himself aloof from most people. His strictness as a parent also made headlines after the publication of his son Gary's book called *Going My Own Way* in 1983. Perhaps these stories have destroyed some of the Crosby luster, but no one can deny his accomplishments in the world of show business.

Crosby was born in 1903 in Tacoma, Washington. His mother was Catherine Harrigan, a true Irish woman, and his father, Harry Crosby, worked as a bookkeeper. They had a large family, five boys and two girls. Bing was the fourth child and his real name was Harry Lillis Crosby. He received the nickname "Bing" from one of the characters in a comic called *The Bingsville Bugle*. The Crosby family moved to Spokane while Bing was still a young boy. There the Crosby boys worked at odd jobs and participated in sports.

Bing also enjoyed singing although he could not read music. He attended a Catholic boys' high school where boxing was his favorite sport. After graduation he went to Gonzaga College in Spokane. Crosby quit school in his junior year to seek a career in show business. He and Alton Rinker, from Gonzaga, traveled to Los Angeles in order to find jobs in their new field. They arrived in L.A. in 1925 and combined talents to form a vaudeville act. Surprisingly, they were successful in securing work and were soon making $65 per week.

Paul Whiteman, the famous bandleader, saw the boys perform and hired the team to work in his organization for $150 per week. Whiteman fans seemed to like the duo until they went East. When they failed to win audiences in New York, Whiteman added Harry Barris to the act and they toured the country as Paul Whiteman's Rhythm Boys. In 1930, the trio appeared in one of Whiteman's early films called *King of Jazz* before differences with Whiteman forced him to fire them.

The trio found some nightclub jobs in L. A. where they caught Mack Sennett's attention. Mack liked Bing's style and signed him to do some movie shorts for him. The films were successful and Crosby began to work as a single. He hired his brother, Everett, to be his business manager and soon Bing had a radio contract for $600 per week with the Columbia Broadcasting System. Bing Crosby made his first broadcast on September 6, 1931. At about that same time he was signed by the New York Paramount Theater to make personal appearances. He was such a hit that he stayed for twenty-nine weeks. As his radio theme song, he used "Where the Blue of the Night Meets the Gold of the Day." Bing, himself, had helped to write the tune.

Along with a rising career, Bing was also enjoying an exciting personal life. Much of this excitement was provided by a new girl friend named Wilma Wyatt (stage name Dixie Lee). The romance blossomed and they were married in 1930. Their family would eventually include four sons: Gary born in 1933, twins Philip and Dennis born in 1934 and Lindsay born in 1938. The Crosby's children would grow up in the San Fernando Valley.

With Bing's success at the Paramount Theater, Paramount Pictures decided to try him in movies and signed him to a contract. His first film was called *The Big Broadcast*. The movie, made in 1932, had a cast recruited from radio shows. In 1933, he was in *Too Much Harmony* with Jack Oakie.

Bing's first big hit film was *Going Hollywood* with Marion Davies, also in 1933. As a result of the popularity of that film he was ranked number four in the 1934 list of Top Ten Box Office Stars.

By 1934 he was recording his songs for a new record company, Decca. Bing would remain with them for all his big recording hits. He would eventually sell over 300 million records, with twenty records selling a million copies or more. His two biggest sellers were both Christmas songs: "White Christmas" and "Silent Night." Most of the songs Crosby chose to record were about happy people or good experiences. He liked tunes that were "up."

Bing made three films in 1934: *We're Not Dressing* with Carole Lombard, *She Loves Me Not* with Miriam Hopkins and *Here Is My Heart* with Kitty Carlisle.

While successfully juggling movie and recording careers Bing signed with Kraft products in 1935 and began his Kraft Music Hall radio show which ran for a decade.

The Crosby film career continued on through the 1930s. His most memorable movies of this period were: *Mississippi* in 1935, *Anything Goes* in 1936, *Sing You Sinners* in 1938 and *East Side of Heaven* in 1939.

Sheet music for the song "May I" from Bing's 1934 Paramount movie, *We're Not Dressing* with Carole Lombard. Mack Gordon and Harry Revel wrote the song. It was published by DeSylva, Brown and Henderson, Inc.

Another Paramount Crosby film for 1934 was *Here is My Heart*. This is a still from the film with Kitty Carlisle as Bing's co-star.

This picture of Bing Crosby was used as advertising for the Harlan Theatre to promote his new picture *Too Much Harmony* in 1933.

In 1935 Bing co-starred with Joan Bennett and W. C. Fields in the Paramount picture *Mississippi*. This still pictures the two young romantic leads in a scene from the film.

In 1938 Crosby, Fred MacMurray, and Donald O'Connor made the successful Paramount picture, *Sing You Sinners*. "I've Got a Pocketful of Dreams" was composed by John Burke and James Monaco. It was published by Santly-Joy-Select.

In addition to making movies and records and doing a weekly radio show, Crosby always had time for sports. In 1935 he became interested in horse racing and started the Bing-Lin-Stables, with Lindsay Howard as his partner. Also as a result of his interest in horse racing, Bing and Pat O'Brien founded the Del Mar race track near San Diego in 1937. An avid golfer, Crosby started the Bing Crosby National Pro-Am Golf Tournament in 1937. Bing always made time in his busy schedule for a round of golf. Many pros said that he would have been good enough for the pro tour if he could have had the time for more practice.

The period of Crosby's greatest film contribution was from 1939-1949. Several of these films were particularly successful because of the chemistry between Bing and one of his co-stars, Bob Hope. The two teamed up for the first time in 1940 when they made the first of the "road" pictures, *Road to Singapore*. The producers at Paramount gave them unheard of leeway when they made the films and let their radio writers add gag lines and ad libs to the prepared script. Dorothy Lamour came along for the ride and the result was just what the country needed: fresh comedy and good entertainment. *Road to Singapore* turned out to be the most popular film of the year. There were seven road pictures in all. The others were: *Road to Zanzibar*-1941, *Road to Morocco*-1942, *Road to Utopia* 1946 (picked as one of the ten best films of the year by the New York Times), *Road to Rio*-1948, *Road to Bali*-1953 (first Technicolor "road" picture), and *Road to Hong Kong*-1962.

Bing Crosby had more movie box office hits during the 1940s than any other performer. They included *Rhythm on the River* in 1940 and *Birth of the Blues* in 1941.

Bing recorded many of the songs from his movies so collectors not only can still see his films via video cassette, they can also collect the records and the sheet music that were released with each movie. Both of these types of collectibles are still relatively inexpensive-perhaps because there are so many from which to choose. One of Bing's most famous songs comes from the *Holiday Inn* movie from 1942, "White Christmas" by Irving Berlin. His recording of this favorite has sold over thirty million copies. A set of paper dolls was also manufactured as a tie-in to the same film. The book featured Bing Crosby and his partner in the film, Fred

Screen Romances for April, 1941 featured the story of the Crosby-Hope hit road picture called *Road to Zanzibar*. Dorothy Lamour also starred.

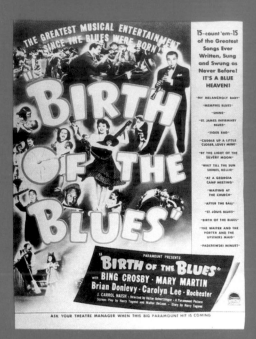

This advertisement is for the Paramount *Birth of the Blues* Crosby film made in 1941. The ad appeared in *Screen Guide* magazine for December, 1941.

In 1942 Hope and Crosby made another successful road picture for Paramount called *Road to Morocco*. Sheet music from the film called "Ain't Got a Dime To My Name" by Johnny Burke and Jimmy Van Heusen. Famous Music Corp. published the music. Dorothy Lamour went along for the ride.

An advertisement from the Paramount Crosby film *Rhythm on the River* with Mary Martin appeared in the *Screen Guide* magazine for September, 1940.

Sheet music for Bing Crosby's most popular hit song, "White Christmas," first used in the 1942 Paramount Pictures film, *Holiday Inn*. Irving Berlin was the composer. The music was published by Irving Berlin, Inc.

Astaire (see chapter on Astaire). Because of the popularity of both stars, these paper dolls are hard to obtain and will be expensive.

During World War II, Bing Crosby, like most Hollywood stars, spent many of his free hours volunteering his help for the war effort. He participated in tours that sold over $14 million worth of war bonds. He entertained the troops wherever possible and covered over 50,000 miles in this endeavor by traveling to England, France and Germany before the war was over.

In 1943 Crosby made his first film in Technicolor. It was called *Dixie* and his co-star was once again Dorothy Lamour. Again Paramount had a hit picture.

But 1944 was to be Bing Crosby's biggest year in pictures. He made a new film called *Going My Way* playing an up-to-date Catholic priest with Barry Fitzgerald portraying an older priest who was set in his ways. Leo McCarey was the director and had also worked out the story. This unlikely casting gave Crosby a chance to do some serious acting for the first time in his career. The film was an astonishing success. It was the fifth biggest hit of the decade. The film received seven Oscars at the Academy Award ceremonies. Bing Crosby received the best actor award, Barry Fitzgerald was honored as best supporting actor and the picture was chosen as best picture of the year. A record album made by Bing Crosby contained the songs from the film.

Because of the movie's huge success, a film sequel called *The Bells of St. Mary's* was planned for 1945. Since Leo McCarey really called RKO his home base, the film was made there with him as director. Crosby's co-star was Ingrid Bergman and again a hit movie was produced. It was the sixth biggest box office film of the decade.

Another musical Crosby picture was made before the end of the war in 1945. It co-starred a new Paramount star, Betty Hutton. The story of the film, *Here Come the Waves* was featured in the *Screen Romances* magazine for February, 1945.

This 78 RPM Decca record album by Bing Crosby featured songs from his Academy Award winning movie, *Going My Way* from 1944.

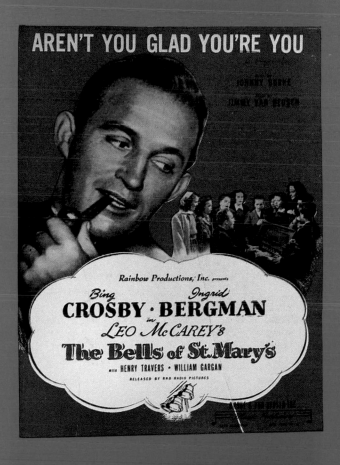

An ad for Bing Crosby's first Technicolor picture, *Dixie* co-starring Dorothy Lamour. The Paramount hit was advertised in *Screen Guide* for August, 1943.

The Bells of St. Mary's was another hit film for Bing Crosby. One of the great tunes from the Rainbow Production was "Aren't You Glad You're You" by Johnny Burke and Jimmy Van Heusen. Burke and Van Heusen published the music in 1945. The movie was released by RKO Pictures.

Screen Romances for February, 1945 featured the new Crosby—Betty Hutton Paramount war-time film called *Here Come the Waves*. The magazine also carried this ad for the film.

One of the popular songs from the Crosby—Astaire hit Paramount film, *Blue Skies* from 1946, was "You Keep Coming Back Like a Song" by Irving Berlin. The music was published by Irving Berlin Music Corp.

After the war, Bing Crosby still had a top rated radio program on NBC. Although he wanted to carry on with the broadcast, he was tired of the weekly hassle. He wanted to record the program so it could be broadcast several times on the same day. At that time, everything was done live and because of the different time zones, sometimes the same show had to be broadcast twice. As a result, the second performance was not always as fresh as the first. Bing wanted to record a forty minute show and then cut out the parts that weren't funny and edit it to a twenty-eight minute program. NBC wouldn't agree to his terms so Bing left them and went to ABC. His first recorded radio show was broadcast on October 16, 1946. It wasn't long before most of the radio shows were done on tape.

Crosby returned to movie musicals when he made *Blue Skies* in 1946. His co-star was again Fred Astaire. There was really not much of a plot but again the Crosby name and the talent of its two stars made the movie very successful.

Bing Crosby was in first place as a box office attraction from 1944-1948 and it wasn't until 1949 when he made *A Connecticut Yankee in King Arthur's Court* that he had less than a hit movie.

Although Crosby had reached his peak as a film star, he still occasionally appeared in excellent films. *Riding High*-1950 and *Here Comes the Groom*-1951 were both successful movies. In 1954 Crosby had another real blockbuster when he made *White Christmas* with Danny Kaye. Once again he sang the famous title song. Television viewers are treated to showings of this film each year and it continues to be a holiday favorite.

A lobby card from the 1950 Paramount movie, *Riding High*, starring Bing Crosby and directed by Frank Capra.

Crosby's hit musical for Paramount from 1954, *White Christmas*, included the song, "Count Your Blessings Instead of Sheep" by Irving Berlin. The music was published by Irving Berlin Music Corp.

Shown is a movie insert from the other hit Crosby film from Paramount, 1954, *The Country Girl* with Grace Kelly.

In 1954 Crosby got another serious acting part when he made the film *The Country Girl* with Grace Kelly. He was praised for his acting, but Kelly received the Oscar, not he.

Bing Crosby and Paramount parted company in 1956 after nearly twenty-five years of film-making. Bing made his last big hit movie for M-G-M in 1956. It was called *High Society* and he starred with Grace Kelly and Frank Sinatra. The film was based on *The Philadelphia Story* with an added musical score. Crosby's last big hit record also came from this movie. It was called "True Love."

Although Crosby continued making films until 1966, he was no longer the top star he had been. He received good notices for his acting in his last film, a remake of *Stagecoach*, but the picture did not do well. Bing Crosby had made sixty films in thirty-five years in his successful movie career. It was time to do other things.

Bing's personal life also began to deteriorate at about the same time as his career was losing its sparkle. His wife, Dixie Lee, first developed a drinking problem and, after a lengthy illness, died of cancer in 1952. The four boys were growing up with difficulty and newspapers were continuously reporting on their misadventures. After several romances with young stars, Bing fell in love with Kathryn Grant (real name Grandstaff) and they were married in 1957. She was twenty-three years old and he was fifty-three at the time of their marriage. The couple had three children: Harry Lillis Jr. born in 1958, Mary Frances (1959) and Nathaniel (1961). The

family settled in Hillsborough near San Francisco and they seemed to be very happy together.

Bing Crosby continued to make television appearances and he always did a Christmas show with his family. In March 1977 he had a bad fall from a stage in a theater in Pasadena when he was rehearsing a television program. He fell twenty feet into the orchestra pit. He seemed to recover from the accident but in October of the same year, he died of a heart attack in Madrid, Spain shortly after finishing a round of golf. His fans were deeply saddened. Bing's voice had provided entertainment for Americans for fifty years. It was hard for his fans to realize he was gone.

Luckily Bing left more of a legacy than most stars. Fans can still delight in watching his entertaining films, listening to his many recordings and can even hear some of his early radio broadcasts.

Because the Crosby career was so varied and lasted for such a long time, there are many Crosby mementoes considered desirable by today's collectors. The more unique items include a Bing Crosby game called *Call Me Lucky* made by Parker Brothers in 1954 and a coloring book published by Saalfield, also from 1954.

Another more valuable memento is his autographed photo pictured here. For a star as successful as Bing Crosby, these movie memories will surely continue to rise in value both in money and in sentiment. Bing Crosby souvenirs can still be called good investments since he was undoubtedly one of the top, if not the top, entertainer of the 20th century.

This *Call Me Lucky* Bing Crosby game was produced by Parker Brothers in 1954. It is a board game that has never been used.

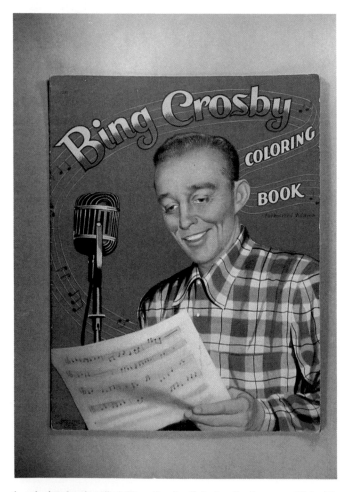

A coloring book called *Bing Crosby Coloring Book* was published by Saalfield Publishing Co. in 1954. The pictures to color are of Bing, his sons, and various Crosby movie scenes.

For fans who are interested in joining a Bing Crosby collector's club, contact:

Club Crosby
P. O. Box 3849
Kirkwood, MO 63122

Membership fee of $10.00 includes semi-annual newsletter of fifty pages.

A Bing Crosby autographed picture is one of the most treasured keepsakes for any Bing Crosby fan. This one was sent to a fan some years ago.

Dionne Quintuplets
Canada's Miracle Babies

Several Dionne Quintuplet collectibles available to collectors. All five composition dolls were made by the Madame Alexander Doll Co. in the mid 1930s. The smaller dolls are 7″ tall, while the larger baby is 10″ tall. The smaller dolls have painted eyes and the baby doll has sleep eyes. All four have molded hair. The larger doll is 20″ tall with sleep eyes, closed mouth and a real hair wig. She has a composition swivel shoulder head, arms and legs and a cloth body. She is marked "Dionne/Alexander". The book was published by Whitman Publishing Co. in 1937 and is titled *Here We Are Three Years Old* .

This booklet called *Administering Angels of the Dionne Quintuplets* tells the story of Madame Legros and Madame Lebel, the midwives who helped deliver the Dionne Quints. The two women are pictured on the cover with the basket which was used as a bed for the tiny quints.

The decade of the 1930s brings memories of dust storms, Apple Annies, soup lines, and farm foreclosures. But it also reminds us of the miracle birth of five identical little girls from Canada. Perhaps it is the remembrance of this happy incident in the midst of the sad depression years that makes collectors so enthusiastic about Dionne Quintuplets memorabilia. Even though the birth took place over fifty years ago near Callander in Ontario, Canada, there seems to be no loss of interest in souvenirs of the famous Dionne Quints.

The babies were born on May 28, 1934 in a small farmhouse, without running water or electricity, to a farm couple with five other children. The doctor had been sent for at the beginning of Elzire Dionne's labor but he had to travel several miles to reach the farm and did not arrive until two of the babies had already been born. A midwife had been in charge until Dr. Allan Roy Dafoe came on the scene. After the unexpected births of the third, fourth, and fifth babies, Dr. Dafoe turned his attention to the mother, a twenty-five year old woman who had given birth to her first child when she was just seventeen years old. She seemed to be near death. A priest was summoned to administer last rites to Mrs. Dionne but by the time of his arrival, she seemed to be improving.

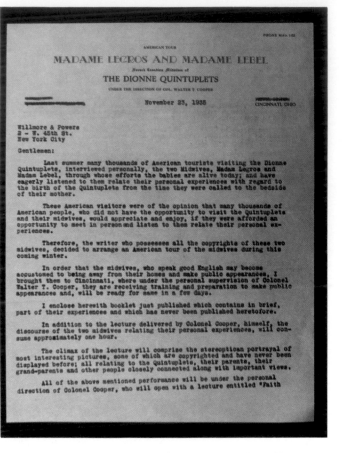

Pictured is a letter from the manager of Legros and Lebel to Willmore and Powers asking for bookings for a lecture tour to be made by the two midwives to capitalize on their involvement with the Dionne births. The letter is dated November 23, 1935.

The babies were not expected to survive, and had been baptized at the time of their births. In order to keep them warm, the underweight infants were wrapped in wool scraps and placed in a basket near the kitchen oven. When Dr. Dafoe had Mrs. Dionne's condition stabilized, he began seeking nursing help for the family. Although there was little hope that the babies would survive, the little ones surprised medical experts and continued to hang on to life. As the news of their births spread, help was offered from everywhere. An old-fashioned kerosene incubator was sent from Chicago. Nurses came from the Red Cross and mother's milk from many different women was secured to feed the children. This service was continued for several months and it played a big part in the babies' survival.

Oliva Dionne, the Quints' father, was overwhelmed by his new family and did not know how he would be able to afford raising this many additional children. He was approached by representatives from the Chicago Century of Progress Exposition who wanted to exhibit the babies at the fair. Seeing a way out of his financial difficulties, he signed a contract agreeing to the proposition. The Canadian people were horrified to think of the babies being exploited in this manner. The government then became involved in the situation by taking control of the babies and a Board of Guardians was appointed to look after their interests. This legal maneuver effectively nullified the Chicago Century of Progress contract.

It is hard to imagine a story like that of the Dionne Quintuplets happening today, but they were born into a different era under very primitive conditions. The largest child weighed only a little

over two pounds and the smallest weighed one pound, eight ounces. Even today, after numerous medical advances, many premature children of those sizes do not live. These babies were born into a family already blessed with several children who would likely spread infection to the tiny babies. It is very unlikely that the Quints would have survived if the government had not intervened.

Louise de Kiriline, an able nurse, was brought to the home to try to organize the situation. She cleaned the front parlor from top to bottom and installed the babies there. She moved the family upstairs and housed the other nurses in the living room. She made sure two of the nurses were on duty at all times and a good part of their time was spent giving the babies eye droppers of mother's milk. The babies were named: Cecile, Yvonne, Marie, Annette and Emilie.

Dr. Dafoe secured the best medical advice he could obtain for the care of the babies. Oxygen was brought in to be used to replace the rum he had been using to stimulate the babies' breathing in emergencies. Several times, one or another of the children had been near death only to be saved by a few drops of rum.

The home situation had to be changed. Too many people lived in the small house and the babies needed more space, air and sunshine. It was agreed that a building would be built across the road to house the babies and the nursing staff so the Dionne's could reclaim their home. In September, the babies were moved to their new quarters even though they were ill with colds. With the new structure and the porch that offered sunshine for the little girls, the babies thrived. By October, when they were five months old, they had weathered the trauma of their births and were well on their way to becoming healthy babies.

This special souvenir section of the *Des Moines Sunday Register* offered readers six pages of pictures of the Dionne babies at the time of their first birthday. The paper was dated June 2, 1935. All pictures were by the NEA Service.

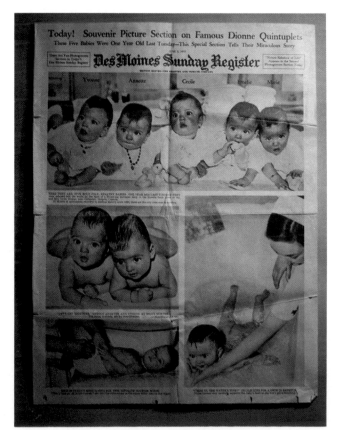

This colored picture is one of the most popular photographs ever published of the Quintuplets. It was sold in all sizes framed and unframed. From left to right: Yvonne, Annette, Cecile, Emilie and Marie.

After the children were installed in their new home, offers to endorse products began to come to the attention of the Board of Guardians. Although Dr. Dafoe was on the board, the father of the Quints was not and he and his wife resented the fact that they were not allowed to have any input into what was happening to their babies. The contract for pictures of the children, which would appear in the world's newspapers, was awarded to the Newspaper Enterprises of America syndicate. Mr. and Mrs. Dionne signed their own picture contract with the New York Daily News so family pictures could not ever be taken in one unit because of the differences in their contract obligations. The Sunday rotogravure sections became an ideal place to show the quints as they grew. By 1936, 672 newspapers were purchasing this material.

The Dionnes, meanwhile, were very unhappy about what was happening to their large family. It had been divided into two parts. The Dionnes lived with their oldest five children in the farmhouse while the newest family members lived across the road in the new hospital with nurses to care for them. It wasn't long until Mr. and Mrs. Dionne began to publicize the fact that they wanted their children returned to them.

As a result of the continued interest in the Quints, a playground was built with a viewing area so that visitors could watch the girls at play. It was finished in time for the 1936 tourist season.

Product endorsements from the Quints began in 1935. The Madame Alexander Doll Co. first started producing the Dionne Quintuplet dolls in that year. Through the years, many different models were made. The first were small 7″ tall all composition baby dolls, then toddlers were added in the 8″ size. When the dolls proved to be good sellers, other sizes were introduced including 12″ to 16″ tall toddler models and a 10″ tall all composition baby doll. A 20″ tall doll with a composition head, arms and legs and a cloth body was also produced. Some of the doll sets included a Dr. Dafoe doll, a nurse doll, or special Quint furniture like swings or a Ferris wheel. These dolls are the most expensive Dionne items for collectors to acquire. The only other doll company allowed to make authorized editions of the Quints was the Superior Co. based in Canada.

This article from the *Des Moines Sunday Register* from September 3, 1935 told why Mr. and Mrs. Dionne did not attend the Quintuplets' first birthday party. The story was titled "Mrs. Dionne Denies Government Has Right to Quintuplets."

A 7½" tall all-composition Madame Alexander Dionne Quint baby doll first made in 1935. She is jointed at the shoulders and the hips with curved baby legs. She has painted features and molded hair. She is all original including her Cecile tag. She is marked on the back of her head "Dionne/Alexander." On the back of her body is marked "Alexander."

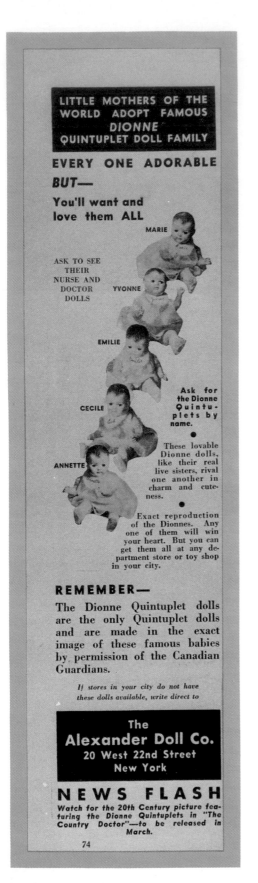
The Madame Alexander Doll Co. began production of Dionne Quint dolls in 1935. This ad appeared in *Modern Screen* magazine for April, 1936.

These 8″ tall all-composition toddler Dionne Quint dolls were also made by the Madame Alexander Doll Co. The dolls have painted eyes and mohair wigs and are jointed at the shoulders and hips. They are all dressed in their original Alexander clothing. They are marked "Dionne/Alexander" on their heads and "Alexander" on their backs.

This 11″ tall set of all-composition toddler Dionne Quint dolls was made by the Madame Alexander Doll Co. The dolls have sleep eyes and painted hair and are jointed at the shoulders and the hips. They are wearing their original pastel dresses and bonnets. They are marked "Alexander" on their heads and "Madame Alexander" on their backs.

This 14″ tall all composition toddler Dionne Quint doll was made by the Madame Alexander Doll Co. She has sleep eyes, closed mouth, and a mohair wig. She is jointed at the hips and shoulders. She is marked "Alexander" on the back of her head and also on her back. She has been redressed.

Paper doll production of the Dionne Quintuplets was also begun in 1935. The authorized editions were made by the Merrill Publishing Co. The first set of paper dolls was called *Quintuplets: The Dionne Babies*. It was number 3488 and contained all five babies in one book.

In 1936, the authorization for paper dolls was purchased by the Whitman Publishing Co. and they manufactured five books, each containing one Quint. They are all numbered 1055. In 1937, the Whitman Co. produced the same paper dolls packaged in a box which included all five girls. The dolls were called, *The Dionne Quintuplet Cut-Out Dolls* and were numbered 2190. Merrill Publishing Co. also produced a set of five separate paper doll books with each book featuring one quint. These books are called *Let's Play House With the Dionne Quints*. They were published in 1940 and were numbered 3500 A, B, C, D, E.

The last set of the Dionne Quint paper dolls was published in 1940, again by the Merrill Co. The quints were pictured in pink slips and showed that they were no longer toddlers but grown-up six-year-olds. The number of the book is 3488. About this same time the Merrill Co. also produced a coloring book called *Dionne Quints: Pictures to Paint* No. 3490.

Other products were also made which carried the Dionne endorsement. These included doll dishes, radios, hair ribbons, little girl's dresses, and handkerchiefs. The handkerchiefs came in several different designs and could be purchased for ten cents each in 1937.

Even sheet music was published to take advantage of the Dionne's popularity, including *Quintuplet Lullaby* with the famous five pictured on the cover. It was published in 1935.

Since the public had taken such a fancy to the Quintuplets, Twentieth Century-Fox decided to secure them for a movie. After favorable negotiations were made with the Board of Guardians, the first Quint movie, *The Country Doctor* was produced in 1935 with Jean Hersholt playing the part of Dr. Dafoe. Dionne Quint pictures were given away at movie theaters to promote the movie. The advertisement was printed on the back of the picture.

A book was published by Grosset and Dunlap in 1936 to tie-in with the new film. It, too was called *The Country Doctor*. The first part of the book told the story of the motion picture while the rest of the book was devoted to the real life of the Dionne Quints. Many pictures of both the movie and the Quints are included in the book.

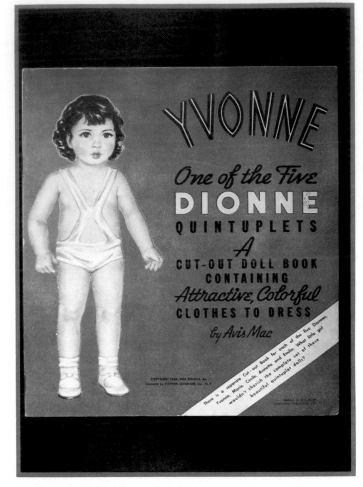

Whitman Publishing Co. produced five individual books of the Quints in 1936. Pictured is the Yvonne book in the series. A car to be punched out is on the back cover.

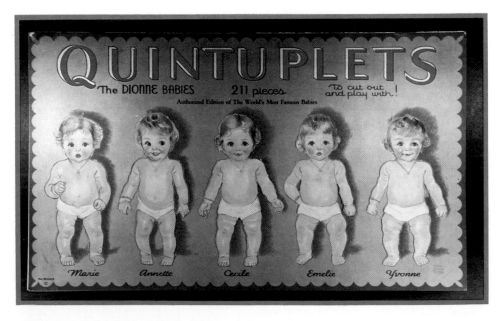

These paper dolls called *Quintuplets: The Dionne Babies* were published by the Merrill Publishing Co. in 1935 and are #3488.

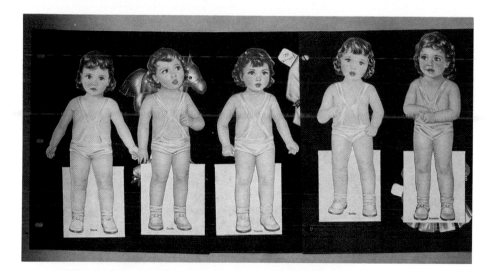

Paper dolls called the *Dionne Quintuplet Cut-Out Dolls* published by Whitman Publishing Co. They were made in 1937 and came boxed. Their number was #2190.

The Merrill Publishing Co. also produced individual Quint paper doll books in 1940. They were numbered 3500 A through E. Pictured is the Cecile booklet. Cardboard furniture to be punched out is featured on the front and back covers.

This coloring book called *Dionne Quints: Pictures to Paint* was published by the Merrill Publishing Co. circa 1940. From the collection of Judy Fitzgibbon Lawson. The photograph was taken by Jean Fitzgibbon Kelly.

The last set of *Dionne Quints Paper Dolls* was published by the Merrill Publishing Co. in 1940, #3488. The babies had grown into little girls but they were still popular with the public.

All of the printed handkerchiefs measure 8½" x 8½."

Mirro aluminum child's dishes were made which featured pictures of the Quints in 1936. The whole set included a setting for six. Each of the Quints was pictured on a plate.

The handkerchiefs were copyrighted by NEA and sold for ten cents each in 1937.

One of the several designs of handkerchiefs which featured pictures of the Dionne Quints.

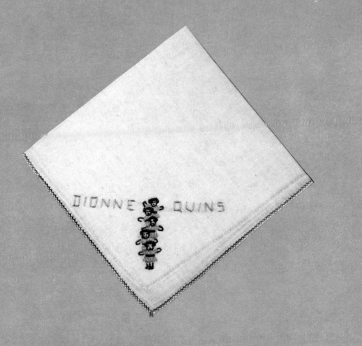

These white handkerchiefs pictured the Quints' images done in embroidery in one corner.

This picture of the Dionne Quintuplets was used with advertising on the reverse side to promote their new motion picture *The Country Doctor*. Courtesy of Savannah Square Mini-Stores, Savannah, Mo.

This *Quintuplets' Lullaby* sheet music was composed by Gordon V. Thompson to honor the Dionne Quints. It was published in 1935 by Leo Feist, Inc.

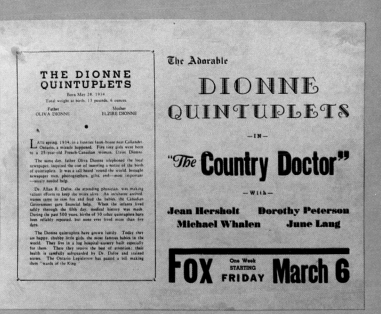

The back side of the picture advertises the first Quint movie, *The Country Doctor* produced by Twentieth Century-Fox in 1936. The movie starred Jean Hersholt playing the part of Dr. Dafoe.

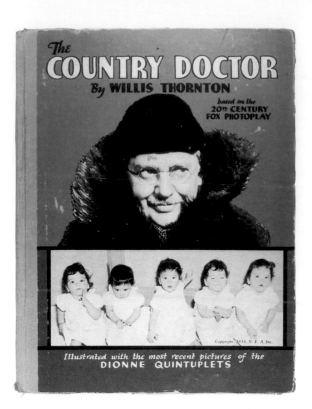

Pictures of the Quints were also used to sell playing cards. Some of the decks of cards also promoted products and some did not.

The Country Doctor book was published by Grosset and Dunlap in 1936. The first part of the book is based on the Quints' first movie and includes pictures and the story line of the film. The last part includes pictures and information about the Quints' real lives.

With the completion of the playground to allow tourists to see the quints, the interest in the little girls reached its peak. The visitors were not charged admission but they did buy souvenirs from the various stands (one owned by the girls' father) and they spent money on food and lodging in Canada as they made the trip. Pennants, postcards and playing cards featuring the Quints' pictures were sold as mementoes to tourists. The Quintuplets became big business. From 1934 until 1943 around three million people visited Quintland. There were two observation periods each day. The first was at 9:30 A. M. and the other was in the afternoon.

The Quints continued to be swamped with requests for endorsements for products. The Karo Syrup ads are especially valued by today's Quint collectors. Most of their ads were in color and one series featured lovely paintings of each individual Dionne Quint.

This postcard pictures the entrance to Callander, the home of the Quints in Ontario, Canada.

This pennant picturing the five little girls was sold at one of the souvenir stands in Callender.

50

Another postcard of the era features the house where the quints were born.

Crowds are pictured in this postcard scene as they line up to view the Quints during their "showing" for the public.

The Dafoe Hospital where the Quints were moved is shown in this old postcard scene.

The home of Dr. Dafoe who delivered the Quints is pictured on this postcard.

In this postcard view, many cars are parked near the souvenir shop of the Quints' father, Oliva Dionne.

This is another scene of Callander as it looked at the time the Quints were bringing tourists to the town. The postcards were all published by Evans and Bowman.

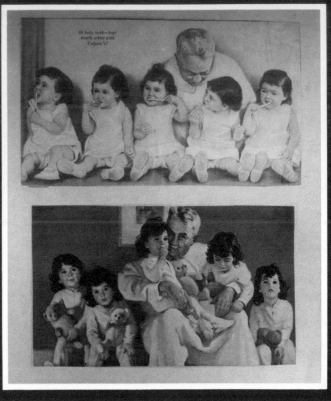

The Quints received quite a lot of money for endorsing products and these ads have become collectible because many of them were in color and are quite attractive. Pictured is an ad for Karo Syrup.

Colgate Toothpaste was also promoted by the Quints. The top scrapbook picture came from one of their ads.

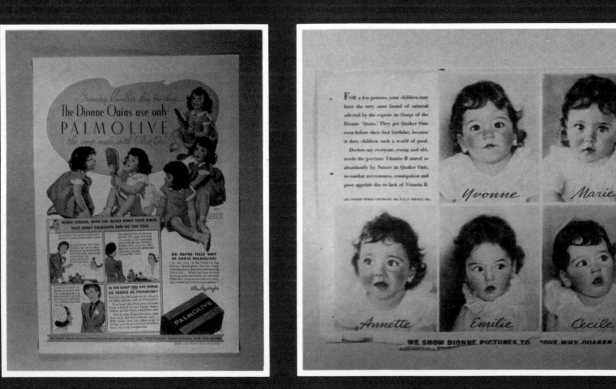

Another product endorsed by the Quints was Palmolive soap as shown in this advertisement.

These pictures of the Quints, from an early scrapbook, were used as an ad for Quaker Oats.

Karo did some especially nice ads using each individual Quint in separate portraits in 1940. The advertisements used paintings by Willy Pogany. Pictured here is Yvonne.

These special ads are probably the favorite for Dionne collectors. Pictured here is the Annette painting.

The same series of ads also featured Marie.

This Karo ad featured a portrait of Cecile.

Pogany also did a nice painting of Emilie for the Karo series.

Their faces also appeared on many items that were used as premiums for various products. These could be secured with box tops or labels from Quint endorsed products. Perhaps the most collectible of these are the spoons made in the image of each girl. The spoons were used as a premium for Palmolive soap in 1939 and customers could purchase each spoon by sending a soap wrapper and ten cents to the company. A metal cereal bowl was also a premium during these years. It was offered by Quaker Oats for ten cents and two trademarks from its product for each bowl. The paper doll book called *All Aboard For Shut Eye Town* was available for three Palmolive wrappers from the Colgate Palmolive Peet Co. in 1937. This book has recently been re-issued. Several booklets featuring the Quints were also produced to promote Lysol products, including "Protecting the Dionnes." Many other Dionne Quint advertising items are available to the collector and they can add interest to a collection.

A very collectible set of the Dionne Quintuplet spoons was made in the late 1930s as premiums for Palmolive Soap. The spoons were manufactured by Carlton Silverplate and each spoon had a figural picture of a different quintuplet on its handle. Each spoon cost ten cents and a soap wrapper when they were ordered by mail in the 1930s. Spoons from the collection of Mary and Ray Baker.

Another premium product picturing the Dionne Quints is this metal cereal bowl with each of the children's features and their names showing on the bowl. It was offered by Quaker Oats for ten cents and two Quaker Oats trademarks.

THE DIONNE QUINTUPLETS DOLLS & COSTUMES CUT-OUT BOOK

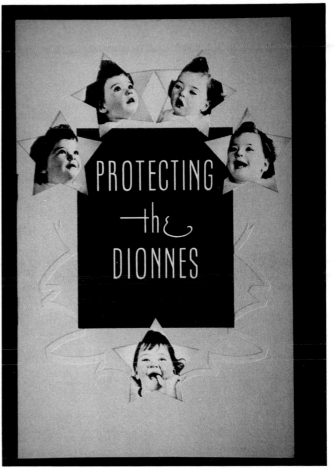

Another premium given away by the Quints' advertisers was the paper doll book called *All Aboard For Shut Eye Town*. The paper dolls were free to consumers for three Palmolive soap labels. In 1984 the Merrimack Publishing Co. re-issued the book under the title *The Dionne Quintuplets Dolls and Costumes Cut-Out Book*.

Pictured is a large grocery display for Quaker Oats from the 1930s which featured the Dionne Quints. Shown with the poster is a set of 8″ Alexander Dionne Quint toddler dolls and a 14″ Alexander Quint toddler. The display is from the collection of Colleen Heidbreder. The dolls and photograph are through the courtesy of Bartine Dickerson.

The Lehn and Fink Products Corp. issued the booklet called *Protecting the Dionnes* in 1936 to promote Lysol. NEA supplied the Quints' photos for the booklet.

With the success of the first movie by Twentieth Century-Fox, a contract was signed to do several more films with the girls. The second film was called *Reunion*. *Photoplay* magazine for December 1936 carried both an ad for the movie and an article on the Dionne Quints. Now that the Quints had become movie stars, they were just as important to movie fans as was the United States' own famous little girl, Shirley Temple. The last film made by the Quintuplets was called *Five Of a Kind* in 1938. Since the last two movies were not as good as *The Country Doctor* and because the girls did not speak English, no other films were made.

The quintuplets still retained their popularity, however, and many firms purchased products picturing the Quints in order to advertise their own businesses. The calendar provided especially good promotional material. Calendars of the girls were produced by the Brown and Bigelow Co. beginning in 1936 and ending in 1955. Fans, too, became popular business giveaways as did blotters and other items.

Books were also published to give the public more information about the Dionnes. *The Story of the Dionne Quintuplets* illustrated here is one of the earliest from 1935. It is stamped "Quintuplets Callander, Canada" so it may have been purchased in their hometown. Although the book was published by the Whitman Publishing Co., the pictures are from the NEA service. Many books were produced as the Quints grew older.

Many of the national magazines made coverage of the Quints part of their regular features since the girls were so popular with the American people. The Quints appeared on the covers of *Woman's Home Companion* (August, 1935), *Modern Screen* (April, 1936, July, 1936, and April, 1937), *Click* (June, 1940), *Life* (May 17, 1937 and September 2, 1940); *Time* May 31, 1937; *Look* (October, 11, 1938), and other magazines of the day.

Photoplay magazine for December 1936 contained an ad for the Quintuplets' new film called *Reunion* to be released by Twentieth Century-Fox at that time.

The Quintuplets in a scene from their Twentieth Century-Fox film, *Reunion* from 1936.

The Quints are posing outside their hospital in this still from their *Reunion* movie.

Another play scene is shown in this still from the *Reunion* movie from 1936.

Articles from the *Photoplay* magazine for December, 1936 and *Movie Mirror* for September, 1936 about the Quintuplets as movie stars.

This movie herald advertised the Quints' last movie, *Five of a Kind* made by Twentieth Century-Fox in 1938. Jean Hersholt again starred in the film.

The Dionne Quintuplet calendars from Brown and Bigelow began with this calendar in 1936. It features an NEA picture from 1935. The G.H. Pearson Hardware store in Clear Lake, Wisconsin distributed this calendar to its customers.

This 1937 calendar was distributed by the Wilder Cafe in Central City, Nebraska. The picture is copyrighted by NEA from 1936.

The caption of the 1938 calendar was "The Five Little Sweethearts of the World." It was also used to advertise the Wilder Cafe.

In 1939 the caption of the calendar was "Five Little Sweethearts... This Year They are Five." The calendar was distributed by Hayes, Sharp and Haggerty Insurance from Rochester, New York.

"School Days" was the caption for the Quint calendar in 1940. It was given away by the Pennington's Mortuary in Hartsville, S. C.

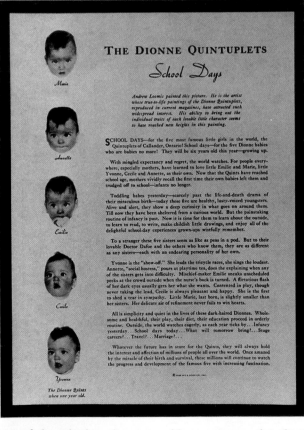

In 1941 the Quints were "All Dressed Up" for their calendar portrait. Missouri Ice Co. of Shelbina, Missouri distributed this calendar.

Many of the calendars also came with an accompanying sheet of information. This one was included with the calendar for 1940. It gives information about Andrew Loomis who did the painting for the calendar as well as data about the Quints themselves.

60

The Missouri Ice Co. also distributed this "Springtime" calendar for 1942. It is one of the nicest of the paintings by Andrew Loomis.

The caption for the calendar for 1943 was "Sunny Days." Again Andrew Loomis did the painting.

In 1944 Loomis used the theme "Maytime" for the Quint calendar. The girls in the picture don't look much like the Dionnes. The Missouri Ice Co. distributed the calendar.

The theme on the Loomis calendar for 1945 was "Harvest Days." The Missouri Ice Co. was the distributor.

In 1947 the Quint calendar was titled "Everybody Helps." This calendar advertises Powers Funeral Home in Oskaloosa, Iowa. The painting was by Loomis.

The Loomis calendar for 1946 was titled "Queens of the Kitchen." Missouri Ice Co. was the advertiser.

The 1948 painting "First Dates" by Andrew Loomis pictures the Quints as if they were getting ready to go out on dates while in reality they still led very sheltered lives. Inter-State Moving and Storage Co. in Kansas City, Kansas used the calendar for advertising.

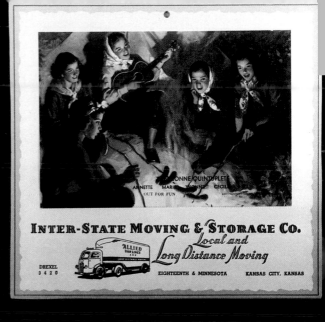

"Fifteen All" was the title of the painting by Andrew Loomis for the calendar for 1949. Again Inter-State Moving and Storage was the advertizer.

The 1951 calendar was called "Out for Fun" again featuring a painting of the girls by Andrew Loomis. Inter-State Moving was the advertizer.

In 1950 Loomis pictured the Quints on horseback but it is doubtful that they ever rode. This calendar was called "Sweet Sixteen" and it was distributed by the Powers Funeral Home in Oskaloosa, Iowa.

The 1952 calendar painting by Loomis looks very little like the real girls. It was called "Smooth Sailing". Inter-State Moving was the advertizer.

The calendar for 1953 had no special caption. It was called "The Dionne Quintuplets". Again the painting was by Andrew Loomis and it was also marked King Features Syndicate, Inc. as were many of the later calendars. Advertising was by Inter-State Moving.

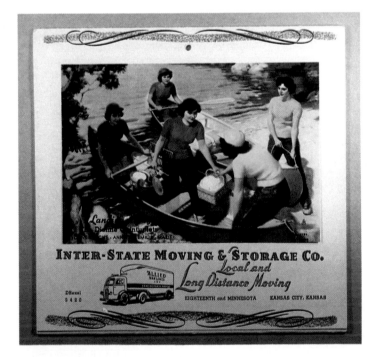

Andrew Loomis continued his fiction Quint calendar art for this 1954 calendar called "Landing Party." King Features was responsible for the copyright and Inter-State Moving was the advertizer.

The last Quint calendar was for 1955. The Loomis painting was called "Grown Up." The calendar was distributed in December, 1954 after the death of Emilie in August of 1954. Since the painting was already finished, the Brown and Bigelow Firm decided to issue the calendar and included an extra sheet explaining that even through Emilie had died, they thought customers would like to have a copy of the last painting ever done of the five girls. Bryant Furniture Co. and Funeral Home in Franklin, North Carolina was the advertiser. The calendar featured small pictures of six of the earlier Dionne Quint calendars.

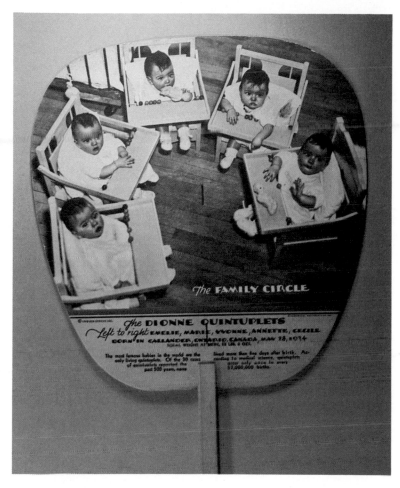

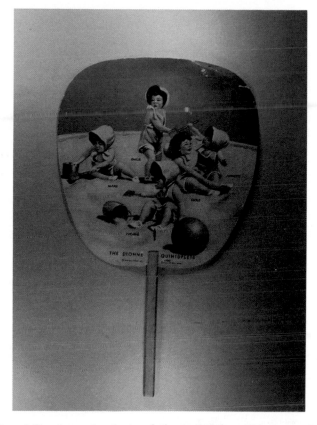

Junge's Bread was advertised on the back of this fan which was also from 1936. NEA Service and Brown and Bigelow are both listed on the fan.

Dionne Quint fans, too, were good products for businesses to issue to customers for promotional purposes. The Brown and Bigelow Co. also manufactured the fans. Many of them featured the Andrew Loomis calendar pictures. The first fan was titled "The Family Circle" and it was made from a 1935 NEA picture.

"Sweethearts of the World" was the title of the fan which pictured all five Dionne Quints. It carries a 1936 NEA Service copyright and this particular fan was used to promote ABC bread.

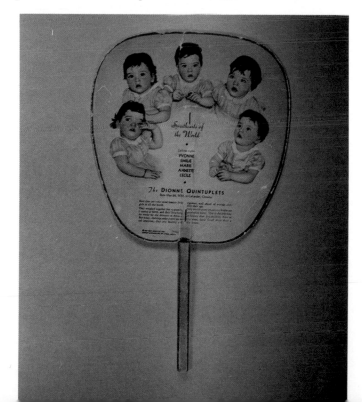

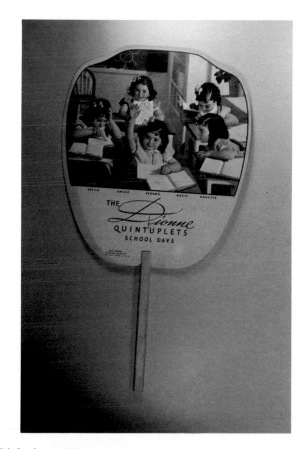

This fan from 1940 repeats the "School Days" calendar theme from 1940. It is by NEA Service and Brown and Bigelow.

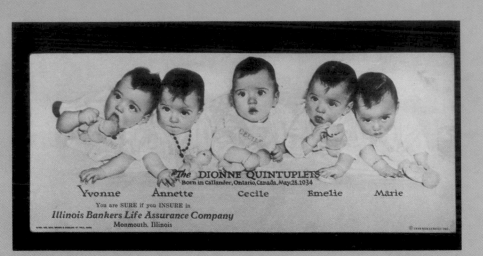

This advertising blotter features the Dionne babies and also promoted the Illinois Bankers Life Insurance Co.

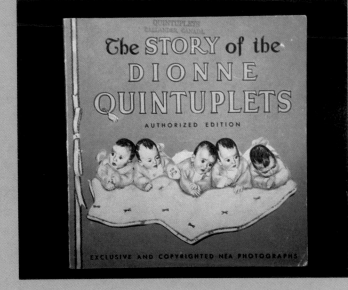

The first book about the Dionne Quints was called *The Story of the Dionne Quintuplets* and was published by the Whitman Publishing Co. in 1935. The photographs were copyrighted by NEA. The book is stamped "Quintuplets/Callander, Canada" so it may have been purchased in their home town.

This book called *The Dionne Quintuplets We're Two Years Old* was published by the Whitman Publishing Co. in 1936. The NEA Service furnished the pictures for all of the books.

The Platt and Munk Co. published this picture book about the Quint babies with pictures by the NEA Service. It was titled *Dionne Quintuplets Growing Up* and is from 1935.

The Dell Publishing Co. produced this book called *Dionne Quintuplets Picture Album* in 1936. It sold for ten cents when it was first marketed.

Whitman Publishing Co. manufactured yet another Quint book in 1936 called *Soon We'll Be Three Years Old* All the books were paperback models.

Here We Are Three Years Old The Dionne "Quins" was again published by the Whitman Publishing Co. in 1937.

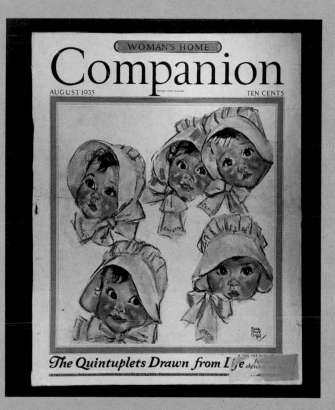

Dionne Quintuplets: Going on Three was also published by the Dell Publishing Co. in 1936. NEA Service supplied fifty pictures for the book.

The Dionne Quintuplets Our Third Year was published by the David McKay Co. in 1937. The pictures were all by the NEA Service.

The first magazine cover for the Dionne Quints came with the August, 1935 issue of *Women's Home Companion*. Instead of a photograph, it was a drawing of the babies by Maud Tousey Fangel.

Click featured a photograph of the girls on its cover in June, 1940 as they celebrated their sixth birthday. An article accompanied the cover feature.

Earl Christy did a painting of the Dionne Quints for the *Modern Screen* magazine April, 1936 cover.

Another nice Quint cover was used by *Modern Screen* in July, 1936. Again the picture was by Earl Christy.

Look magazine for October 11, 1938 featured the Quints and Dr. Dafoe on the cover. The inside article pictured a model showing costumes from the Quint film called *Five of a Kind*.

By the time of the *Life* cover from 1940, the Quints had made a good deal of money and they were worth nearly a million dollars. Their movies, alone, had brought them around $400,000. Much of the money had to be spent for their upkeep because it cost nearly $50,000 per year to run the establishment where they lived, including the salaries of all the employees.

Dr. Dafoe, too, was making lots of money from his connection with the Dionne girls. He was paid for personal appearances, product endorsements, and his Columbia Broadcasting System radio show three mornings each week. *Lysol* disinfectant sponsored the program and also distributed booklets on child care featuring Dr. Dafoe.

As the Doctor gained personal fame, the rift between the Dionne family and Dr. Dafoe widened. In 1941, Mr. Dionne decided the girls could only speak French, even though the Doctor spoke only English. On a Canadian radio program in 1941, the children would not perform in English and would only say their parts in French. The government finally gave in and made plans to return custody of the children to their parents. A new larger house had to be built, however, before the family could be reunited.

Dr. Dafoe resigned from his Quint position in February, 1942 and he died a little more than a year later, still estranged from the Dionne family.

Emergency Aids While Waiting for the Doctor is a booklet by Dr. Allan Roy Dafoe. This advertising item was distributed by Lehn and Fink Products (Lysol) in 1938. Besides advice, it also featured several pictures of the Quints.

The Country Doctor Talks to Women was another booklet by Dr. Allan Roy Dafoe. It was published in 1937 and was another Lysol give away. Excerpts from Dafoe's CBS radio show and pictures of the Quints were included in the booklet.

The Dionnes began the effort to reunite their family during the construction of the new house. The Quints were expected to come to Sunday dinner each week in their parents' home and they attended school with their brothers and sisters in the hospital building daily.

The big house was finished in November, 1943 (prolonged because of the war and the scarcity of materials) and the family was under one roof for the first time in nearly nine years. It did not seem to be a happy arrangement. The nine year-old Quints had been raised as little princesses while their siblings had been treated like ordinary children. Resentment couldn't help but be present. Chores were given to the five girls for the first time in their lives and they were unhappy to be doing what they considered to be more work than that assigned to their siblings. The love for parents and other relatives that grows naturally in most children from childhood was expected to occur immediately in the Quints. The reunion, itself, did not create a sense of family. The Quints had been outsiders for too long. Their closest ties still were to each other and the rest of the Dionne family resented that.

Perhaps if the girls had been reunited with their family at a much earlier age, their lives might have developed differently but too many years had passed for the breach to heal. The united family the Dionnes had hoped for was never achieved.

The girls continued to attend their own private school until they finished high school and then in 1952 they were allowed to go away to college at the age of eighteen. During the next few years, Marie, Yvonne and Emilie all considered a life in religious service but none of them completed their vows to become nuns. The girls' education and life experiences had not really prepared them for the outside world. Yvonne and Cecile did complete nurses' training but health problems prohibited them from proceeding with their careers.

Tragedy struck the Quintuplets in 1954 when Emilie died during an epileptic seizure in a convent in St. Agathe. She was apparently suffocated by her bed pillow when a seizure struck and she could not move her head. She had first started having the seizures when she was twelve years old but the medical problem had been kept a secret from the public.

Annette married Germain Allard in 1957 and after the birth of three children they were divorced. Cecile married Philippe Langlois soon after and four children were born to this couple before their divorce. Marie married Florian Houle in 1958 and she became the mother of two daughters before their separation. Yvonne remained single. Marie, who had been the smallest of the Quints at birth, continued to be plagued with poor health and died in 1970, apparently from a blood clot to the brain.

In the 1970s the three surviving sisters moved to a suburb of Montreal to remain in close touch. Money became a problem for single mothers Cecile and Annette who had been using their trust funds to support their families. Yvonne was in better circumstances because she had not had the additional expense of a family. Cecile worked as a grocery clerk for a time to supplement her income and Yvonne worked as a librarian.

The girls never were reconciled to their family. In 1965 they wrote a book called *We Were Five* in which they expressed their displeasure with the way they were treated by their parents. Publication of the book only served to widen the rift.

A later book by Pierce Berton was also written about the Quint phenomenon. It is called *The Dionne Years* and it has also become a collectible for Quint collectors.

As collectors pursue the Dionne Quint memorabilia from happier times, they have to pause to consider how all the hoopla that produced the Quint products also contributed a later life time of unhappiness for Marie, Emilie, Yvonne, Annette and Cecile. The scale of justice does not balance in the Quints' favor.

For interested collectors:

Dionne Quint Collectors
P. O. Box 2527
Woburn, MA 01888

$10 per year for Quarterly Newsletter

Dionne Quints Home Museum
Seymour Street and Highway 11 South
North Bay, Ontario
Canada

This early Dionne Quint scrapbook contains pictures and clippings from *The Evening World-Herald* from Omaha, Nebraska dated May 25, 1944. The newspaper ran a feature on the Quints and their large family as they lived in the "Big House."

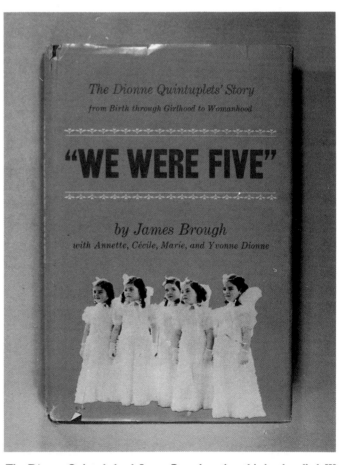

The Dionne Quints helped James Brough author this book called *We Were Five* in 1965. Because of the way they described their relationship with their family, they caused family dissention that never healed. The book was published by Simon and Schuster.

Another later book about the Dionnes has also become a collectible. It is titled *The Dionne Years* by Pierce Berton and was published by W. W. Norton and Co. in 1977.

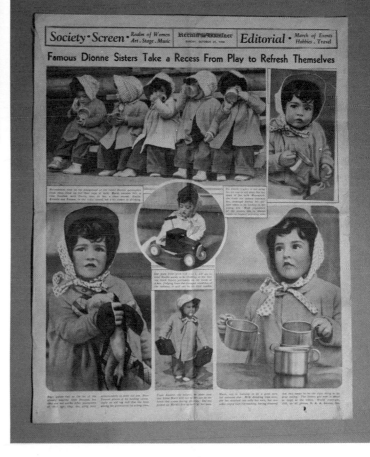

The *Omaha Herald-Examiner* offered its readers glimpses of the Quints in color on October 25, 1936.

Deanna Durbin
Everybody's Sweetheart

This still of Deanna Durbin is marked on the back "Deanna Durbin/15 year old singing star of/New Universal Pictures."

Deanna Durbin was one of the most popular teenage stars of all time. She retired from public life in 1950 at the age of twenty-seven and, shunning publicity and comeback invitations, lives privately in France. As a result, her fans still picture her as a teenager, a memory the star apparently wants to foster.

Miss Durbin made twenty-one films during her career. At the height of her fame, in 1945 and 1947, Deanna was the highest paid woman star in Hollywood, earning $300,000 a year.

Deanna Durbin was born in Winnipeg, Canada in 1922 as Edna Mae Durbin. She and her parents soon moved to Los Angeles where it was discovered she had an unusually remarkable singing voice for a child.

In 1935, she was signed by Metro-Goldwyn-Mayer studios and made a short film called *Every Sunday* with another newcomer to M-G-M, Judy Garland. Part of this short was included in the M-G-M film, *That's Entertainment*, produced in 1974. After Miss

Durbin was at M-G-M for six months, Louis B. Mayer told his associates to terminate one of the girls. Legend has it that he meant to get rid of Judy and dropped Deanna by mistake.

After losing her M-G-M contract, she then began singing on the Eddie Cantor radio show and became very popular with the public. Universal Pictures was in financial trouble at this time, and Joe Pasternak was on the lookout for promising new talent that might bring prosperity to the studio. Because of her radio success, he decided to take a chance on Deanna and signed her to a contract. Her first film for the studio, *Three Smart Girls* in 1936, grossed $2 million and Universal Pictures was saved. In her second film, the 1937 hit, *One Hundred Men and a Girl* she sang while Leopold Stokowski conducted the orchestra. Her salary escalated to $3,000 per week plus an extra $10,000 for each film. Some of

Sheet music from the Universal movie, *Mad About Music* from 1938. The song is called "I Love to Whistle" by Jimmy McHugh and Harold Adamson. The music was published by the Robbins Music Corp. and copyrighted by the Universal Music Corp.

the Universal Pictures' publicity about their new singing star included stills like the one shown.

Deanna's fantastic career continued to skyrocket through 1938. She made two films that year: *Mad About Music* and *That Certain Age*. Her work was recognized by the Hollywood community when she was awarded a miniature Academy Award in 1938 for "bringing to the screen the spirit and personification of youth."

Fans of all ages enjoyed the young girl's beautiful singing voice and her likable personality. Little girls, particularly, identified with the teenage star and a whole line of products was produced using Miss Durbin's image. Perhaps the most sought after item for present day collectors is the Deanna Durbin doll made by the Ideal Novelty and Toy Co. in 1938. The all-composition doll has sleep eyes and an open mouth with teeth. Most models had wigs of human hair, although a few were wigged in mohair. She was made in sizes of 14″, 17″, 21″ and 25″. The doll is highly valued today with its price depending on the doll's size and the condition of both the original clothing and the doll itself.

Paper dolls, too, were produced to honor the new singing star. The Merrill Publishing Co. made two different sets of these paper products, one in 1940: #3480 and one in 1941: #4804. Little girl's dresses, hats, children's books and coloring books were also produced with the star's endorsement. The coloring books were published by the Merrill Co. in the early 1940s. One was *Deanna*

Pictured is a 21″ tall all-composition Deanna Durbin doll with an open mouth and teeth. She has sleep eyes, a real hair wig and is wearing her original dress. She was made in 1938 and is marked on the back of her head "Deanna Durbin/Ideal Doll." On her back is "Ideal Doll."

This composition doll was made by the Ideal Novelty and Toy Co. The doll is 17″ tall, with a real hair wig, sleep eyes, open mouth with teeth, and is dressed in her original clothing. She is marked "Deanna Durbin" on her back but she is wearing the same style dress worn by Judy Garland dolls marketed by the Ideal Co. in the early 1940s. It is certain that Ideal used the same body with different heads for both dolls. This doll may have been intended to represent Judy Garland even though it is marked "Deanna Durbin."

Durbin No. 3479 from 1940 and the other was *Deanna Durbin and Her Trunk Full of Clothes*, No. 4805 from 1941. Even items as common as school tablets sold better when Deanna's picture graced the cover.

In the meantime, Miss Durbin continued making two hit pictures each year and her popularity endured. In 1939, Universal Pictures released *Three Smart Girls Grow Up* and *First Love* with Bob Stack. In the latter film, Miss Durbin received her first screen kiss. The same year a song book was published by G. Schirmer, Inc. called *Deanna Durbin's Favorite Songs and Arias*. The book also featured several pictures from Deanna's films.

While 1940 marks the end of Deanna's teenage idol period of film making, she did star in two films that year, *It's a Date* and *Spring Parade*. Although movie poster material for Deanna's earliest movies is quite expensive, lobby cards from her later films can usually be found at a reasonable price. The Durbin pictures for 1941 included *It Started With Eve* and *Nice Girl*.

Dolls from a two doll paper doll book published by the Merrill Publishing Co. in 1941. The number is 4804.

These paper dolls of Deanna Durbin date from 1940. Three different dolls are featured and the set was made by the Merrill Publishing Co. The number is 3480.

Whitman Publishing Co. produced a series of fiction books with movie stars playing a role in the action. This one called *Deanna Durbin and the Feather of Flame* was published in 1941. Another title was *Deanna Durbin and the Adventure of Blue Valley*.

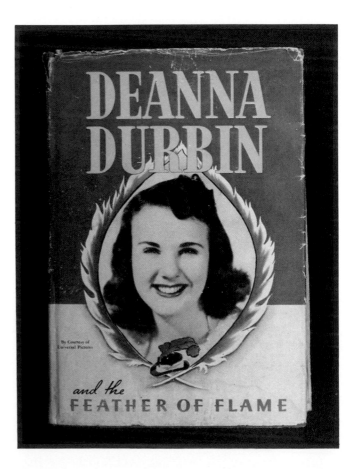

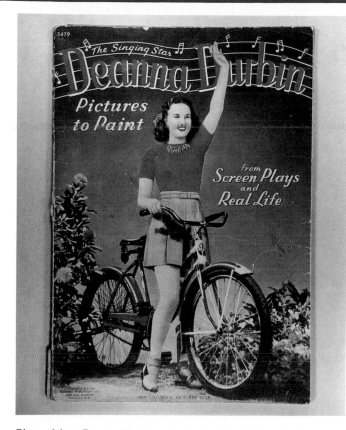

Pictured is a *Deanna Durbin* coloring book published by the Merrill Publishing Co. in 1940. The number is 3479.

A school tablet circa 1940 featuring Deanna Durbin's picture on its cover. It is marked "Movies/Deanna Durbin © Litho U.S.A."

Deanna Durbin and Her Trunk Full of Clothes is a coloring book, number 4805. The book was published by the Merrill Publishing Co. in 1941.

Deanna Durbin's Favorite Songs and Arias was published by G. Schirmer, Inc. in 1939. The book also featured several pictures from Deanna's films.

Sheet music from the Universal Deanna Durbin film, *It's a Date* from 1940. The song, "It Happened in Kaloha" was by Ralph Freed and Frank Skinner. It was published by the Robbins Music Corp.

Sheet music of the song, "Thank You America" from Deanna's Universal movie, *Nice Girl* in 1941. The song is by Walter Jarmann and Bernie Grossman. The music was published by Remick Music Corp.

Pictured is a lobby card featuring Deanna Durbin and the cast from the Universal picture *Spring Parade* which was made in 1940.

Deanna Durbin was a favorite with the fan magazines and her picture graced many of the covers of these publications during both the late 1930s and the early 1940s. But, as she grew up, Deanna began to experience the problems of other adult stars. She married Vaughn Paul, a Universal director, at the age of eighteen and then divorced him in 1944 while he was in the service during World War II. Her public had difficulty adjusting to a grownup Deanna Durbin. Their teenage star becoming a divorcee was a little hard for the fans to accept.

She also had a dispute with Universal Pictures and stayed off the screen for six months after her marriage. As a result, only one Durbin movie was released during the period. It was *The Amazing Mrs. Holliday* and the film was featured in pictures in the *Movie Show* magazine, November, 1942. The film was still called *Forever Yours* at that time.

By 1943, Deanna Durbin had successfully made the difficult transition, as a film actress, from child to adult roles but she was never again to achieve the success she had won as a teenager. During that year she made *His Butler's Sister*, and *Hers to Hold*, co-starring Joseph Cotton. Durbin's pictures ceased to be strictly musicals and she began playing dramatic roles, sometimes singing a song or two during the course of the movie.

Deanna was still receiving her share of movie covers in 1944 when she made *Christmas Holiday* for Universal. The film was a sordid crime story with Deanna involved in wrong doing as she helped her husband-killer played by Gene Kelly. Many of her fans did not approve of this kind of role for their "girl next door." One of the hit songs of the year was "Always" which was featured in the movie. Deanna also made a full-fledged musical in 1944, but it is not now considered to be as good as *Christmas Holiday*. It was called *Can't Help Singing* and sheet music from the picture is shown here. This was Deanna's first Technicolor film.

Fan magazines which featured Deanna Durbin on covers included *Screen Album* for Winter, 1938.

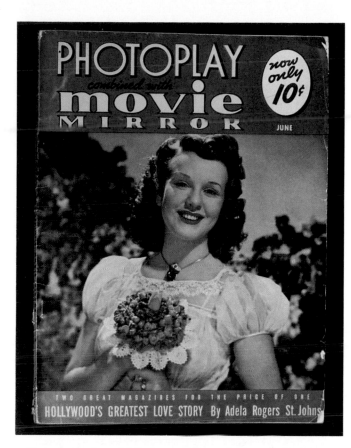

Photoplay for June, 1941 also used Deanna's photo on its cover.

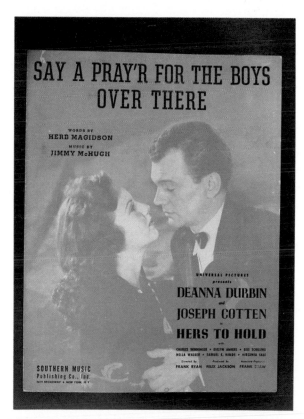

Sheet music from Deanna's 1943 Universal movie, *Hers to Hold*. The song was a popular World War II number, "Say a Pray'r for the Boys Over There." The lyrics are by Herb Magidson and the music is by Jimmy McHugh. Southern Music Pub. Co. published the music.

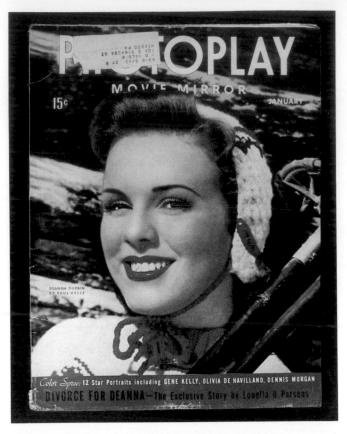

Movie magazines were still featuring Deanna Durbin on covers in January, 1944 when *Photoplay* pictured the star in a winter pose.

Deanna's first Technicolor film in 1944, *Can't Help Singing* (made by Universal) featured this song called "More and More" by Jerome Kern and E. Y. Harburg. It was published by T. B. Harms Co.

A new marriage to Felix Jackson in 1945 and her daughter Jessica's birth in 1946 kept Deanna off the screen for nearly a year. When she resumed her film making, her career had lost speed. Miss Durbin was still drawing a large salary from Universal but was no longer a top box office attraction. Her next film was called *Lady On a Train*. This movie was very important in Deanna's life as her next husband, Charles-Henri David, was the director of the picture. The film is also considered to be a very good mystery.

Miss Durbin's other Universal films from the 1940s included: *Because of Him* (1946), *Something in the Wind* (1947), *I'll Be Yours* (1946), *Up In Central Park* (1948) and *For the Love of Mary* in 1949. Before the release of her last film in 1949, Miss Durbin's studio announced that they were releasing her from her contract since she was no longer able to draw the public to her films. Universal did pay her for the three additional movies she was to have made for them.

Instead of trying another studio, Deanna Durbin retired from films. She was only twenty-seven years old. She had been in the movie business for over half of her life.

After her second divorce, she married French director Charles-Henri David in 1950 and moved to France. Their son Peter Henry was born in 1951. In the French village, Neauphie-le-Chateau located near Paris, Miss Durbin has lived happily and privately with her husband and two children.

Deanna has refused offers of public appearances and comebacks, preferring to be remembered as she once was-a remarkable, talented young lady. Miss Durbin is gracious to fans, however, and still signs autographs for her admirers.

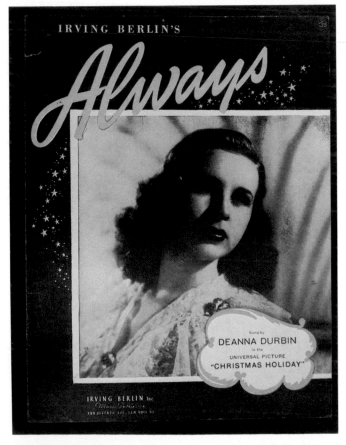

The Durbin Universal movie, *Christmas Holiday* from 1944 also featured a famous song from the war years, "Always" by Irving Berlin. The music was published by Irving Berlin, Inc.

Sheet music from the Universal-Durbin film, *Something in the Wind* featuring "The Turntable" song by Leo Robin and Johnny Green. It was published by the Miller Music Corp. and was copyrighted by the Universal Music Corp. The movie was released in 1947.

"It's Dreamtime" sheet music from the Universal Durbin film, *I'll Be Yours* from 1946. The music is by Walter Schuman and the lyrics are by Jack Brooks. The sheet music was published by Santly-Joy Inc.

This autographed picture of Deanna Durbin David, was signed after her retirement in France.

Clark Gable

The King

Clark Gable received a lot of publicity when he enlisted in the army at the age of forty-one. This *Screen Guide* cover story for February, 1944 concentrated on his war record.

Clark Gable died on November 16, 1960 at the age of fifty-nine. He had been known as the "King of Hollywood" for nearly thirty years and no actor has come along since his death to claim the title. Gable was an original. He appealed equally to movie fans of both sexes. To the men, he represented the masculine outdoor hero most of them dreamed of being. To the women, he was appealing because he was tough but gentle and, of course, had tremendous sex appeal.

Gable collectors have a wealth of material from which to choose because of the longevity of his career. The star made over sixty-five movies during a period of thirty years. From 1932-1942 he was among the top ten money making stars in Hollywood. His World War II service interrupted his career but after his return, he was again ranked as one of the top ten male stars in 1945, 1947, 1949, and 1955.

He was born William Clark Gable in 1901 in Cadiz, Ohio. During his youth he worked in factories and oil fields before he became interested in the theater. He performed in stock theatre and a tent show before he went to Portland and joined a little theater group. Josephine Dillon was the director and even though she was much older than Gable, they were married in 1924. The couple moved to Los Angeles where Gable did some work in silent films, and then they went on to New York. After a futile effort to secure stage work in New York, Clark returned to Los Angeles. With the help of Lionel Barrymore he landed a role in his first talking picture in 1931 for Metro-Goldwyn-Mayer. It was called, *The Painted Desert*. He appeared in twelve films in 1931, and in many of them he was the leading man. In 1932, he became a major star when he played opposite Jean Harlow in *Red Dust*.

By this time, Gable's basic screen character had been established and he continued to play him in all his films. The character was just as good in a modern setting as in a period piece. As long as adventure and/or women were involved with the story line, Gable's character was effective. Even when Gable played a heel in his movies, he never lost his audience appeal. His impish grin, cocky manner, and great screen charisma made even the most ordinary film a box office winner.

As Clark's career became more important, his marriage seemed to matter less, and he and Dillon were divorced. Gable could never seem to remain single for long and he soon made the second of his five marriages. This time the bride was Ria Langham, another older woman, but blessed with money.

The King was well on his way to stardom when several films, including another Jean Harlow hit called *Hold Your Man*, were released in 1933. In 1934, M-G-M loaned him to Columbia to make a little comedy called *It Happened One Night*. The film turned out to be a blockbuster, winning Academy Awards for best picture, for Gable as best actor, for his co-star Claudette Colbert as best actress, and for Frank Capra as best director. A small book was published by Saalfield in 1935 that shows many scenes from the popular film.

In 1935, there were several memorable Clark Gable pictures including *China Seas* (again with Jean Harlow), *Call of the Wild* and *Mutiny on the Bounty* with Charles Laughton.

Gable's films for 1936 continued his run of hits with the popular *San Francisco* co-starring singing star Jeanette MacDonald and *Cain and Mabel* with Marion Davies. Although Gable was never a musical star, he did appear in several musicals.

After 1936, Clark Gable slowed down his film career somewhat and limited himself to two films each year from 1937-1939. The next blockbuster film for Gable was the 1939 movie, *Gone With*

Title song sheet music from *Hold Your Man*, an early Clark Gable—Jean Harlow film made for Metro-Goldwyn-Mayer in 1933. The music is by Herb Brown and the lyrics are by Arthur Freed. The music was published by Robbins Music Corp. in 1933.

An ad for M-G-M's *China Seas* was included in *Screen Book* for September, 1935. The film starred Gable with Jean Harlow as his co-star.

This *It Happened One Night* book is similar in format to the Big Little Books. It was published by Saalfield Publishing Co. in 1935 and pictures many scenes from the Columbia Academy Award winning movie.

the Wind. Nearly every reader of Margaret Mitchell's novel considered Gable the only actor to portray the Rhett Butler character. David Selznick, who was making the movie, was forced by public opinion to secure the services of Clark Gable for the role. In order to do that, he had to give M-G-M (run by his father-in-law Louis B. Mayer) distribution rights to the film as well as a share of the profits. It was a high price to pay but the end result proved the public was right.

Gable did not really want the part. He was afraid he would not be able to live up to the fans' expectations. His second marriage was on the rocks and he was romantically involved with the screwball comedy star, Carole Lombard. If rumors are to be believed, he was induced to take the part with money to be used to buy his divorce from his second wife, Ria Langham.

The movie was a huge success and Gable collectors have a bonanza of GWTW memorabilia from which to choose. Two sets of paper dolls were published by Merrill in 1940 in the images of the stars of the film. One book of dolls had eighteen figures of the major cast members, while the other set contained two each of Rhett and Scarlett and one of Carreen O'Hara. These paper dolls are among the most collectible of any sets of paper dolls and as a result they are expensive. Movie programs and books from the film are also highly collectible.

Sheet music of "Would You" from the M-G-M film *San Francisco* with Jeanette MacDonald as Gable's co-star. The song was by Arthur Freed and Nacio Herb Brown. It was published by Robbins Music Corp. in 1936.

These *Gone With the Wind* paper dolls were produced by the Merrill Publishing Co. in 1940. The set contained eighteen dolls and included most of the featured players. The number was 3404.

Marion Davies was featured with "The King" in a 1936 film for Warner Brothers from 1936 called *Cain and Mabel*. The pictured sheet music from the film is called "I'll Sing You a Thousand Love Songs". It is by Harry Warren and Al Dubin and was published by Remick Music Corp. in 1936.

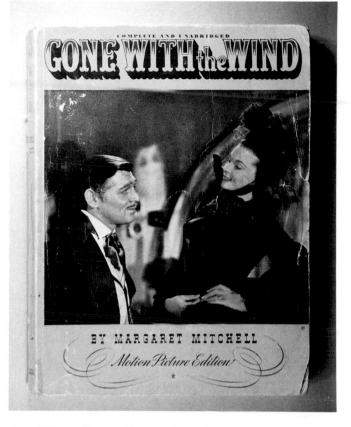

Another set of *Gone With the Wind* paper dolls was published containing only five dolls. Besides Gable and Vivien Leigh, Ann Rutherford was also shown in paper doll form. This Merrill publication was also produced in 1940 and is numbered 3405. An exact replica of this paper doll book was published in 1989 by The Turner Store in Atlanta, Georgia to mark the fiftieth anniversary of the *Gone With the Wind* movie. It is pictured here.

Gone With the Wind by Margaret Mitchell was published in a motion picture edition, featuring scenes from the movie, by Macmillan Co. in 1940.

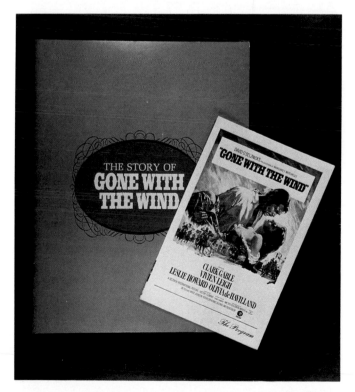

This *Gone With the Wind* program for the David O. Selznick film was distributed to patrons during the 1967 release of the film. Also for sale at the theater was the booklet called *The Story of Gone With the Wind* by Bob Thomas, published by National Publishers Inc. It sold for $1.00.

New products are still being made to represent the famous film characters. A Clark Gable doll in his role as Rhett Butler was made in 1986 by the World Doll Co. The doll is 21″ tall and made of vinyl. To commemorate the fiftieth birthday of *Gone With the Wind* in 1989 many more new collectibles were produced. Although the movie won ten Oscars, Clark Gable did not win. It is still hard to understand why he was passed over. This role was the peak of the Gable career.

Clark Gable continued to make films and most of them did very well at the box office. He played in *Boom Town* in 1940 with Spencer Tracy, Hedy Lamarr, and Claudette Colbert, which was a great success. *Honky Tonk* in 1941 began a series of films with Gable starring opposite one of M-G-M's fastest rising stars, Lana Turner. They continued the winning combination in 1942 in *Somewhere I'll Find You* and again, after the war, in *Homecoming* in 1948.

Because of the interest of fans in movie stars' personal lives, a small industry grew up in Hollywood to publicize the location of major star's homes and Clark's residence became a popular attraction for tourists. The fans purchased maps so they could drive by their favorite actor's mansion. Bus trips were also arranged to take tourists directly to the houses and fans were encouraged to purchase postcards on their trip. Gable's home was pictured in several postcards views.

Clark Gable divorced his second wife in 1939 and married Carole Lombard. They seemed to be very happy together. She looked after him and shared his interest in his outdoor life at their ranch. Some believe Carole was Gable's "true love." Tragedy struck in 1942 when she was killed in a plane crash while on a

World War II bond selling drive. Gable was grief stricken and could not seem to get over her death. *Modern Screen* for June, 1942 devoted its cover to a memorial to Carole.

Even though Clark Gable was forty-one years old and in no danger of being drafted, he took his grief with him and joined the army. The fan magazines followed his career with interest and did several stories on his service activities. Gable eventually was promoted to major and made several missions over Europe before he was assigned to produce training films. He was awarded the Distinguished Flying Cross before he became a civilian again in 1945.

With his return to film making-the phrase, "Gable Is Back and Garson's Got Him" was invented to promote his new film with Greer Garson called, *Adventure*. The jingle didn't help. The film was not a good one. In 1947, he did have a fine role in the hit movie, *The Hucksters* but most of his other films were mediocre like *To Please a Lady* opposite Barbara Stanwyck. This 1950 film was featured in *Movie Story* in November, 1950.

A lobby card from the 1940 M-G-M movie, *Boom Town*. Gable's co-stars were Spencer Tracy, Hedy Lamarr, and Claudette Colbert.

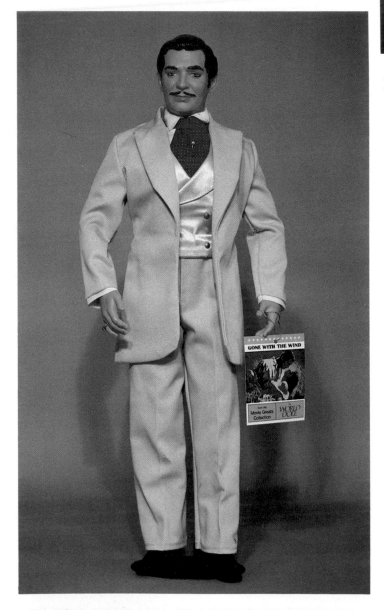

This 21″ tall vinyl doll represents Clark Gable in his role of Rhett Butler in *Gone With the Wind*. The doll is by World Doll Co. from 1986. A companion doll of Vivien Leigh as Scarlett was also made.

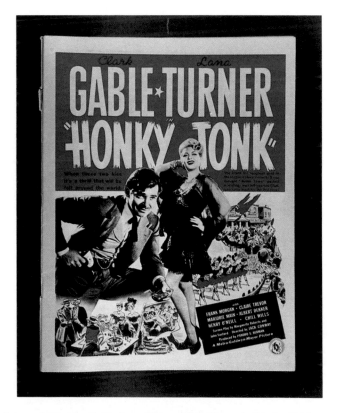

A large ad for the Gable-Lana Turner M-G-M movie *Honky Tonk* was featured in the *Screen Guide* magazine for November, 1941.

Another film with Gable and Lana Turner as co-stars was *Homecoming* made by M-G-M in 1948. This is a still from that film.

Clark Gable and Lana Turner were pictured on the cover of the *Family Circle* magazine for September 11, 1942 to promote their new M-G-M movie called *Somewhere I'll Find You*.

This postcard of Clark Gable's home was manufactured by the Longshaw Card Co. in the 1930s.

Modern Screen devoted its cover for June, 1942 to Carole Lombard in a tribute to the late star. She was Gable's wife at the time of her death in an airplane crash.

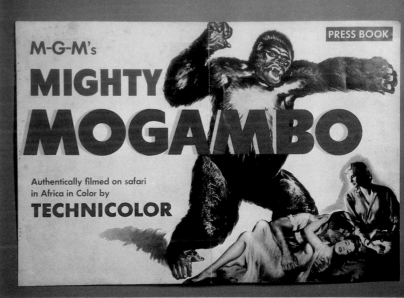

Gable did a remake of his earlier *Red Dust* film in 1953. The film was called *Mogambo* and co-starred Grace Kelly and Ava Gardner. Shown is the press book for the movie.

Movie Story for November, 1950 did a feature on the movie *To Please a Lady* which starred Gable and Barbara Stanwyck.

After the war, Gable was married for the fourth time. His new bride was Lady Sylvia Ashley. The marriage did not last and they were divorced in 1952. In 1955 he was married for the fifth and last time to Kay Williams Spreckles and for the first time since his marriage to Carole Lombard, he seemed to be truly happy.

In 1953, Gable did something no other star had done. He remade a film he had made twenty years earlier *(Red Dust)* and still played the same romantic lead with a new generation of co-stars (Ava Gardner and Grace Kelly). The movie, called *Mogambo,* scored another hit for its star.

Gable continued making movies throughout the 1950s, but at a slower pace. He never had a time in his long career when he was off the screen for over a year except when he was in the service during World War II. He left M-G-M in 1954 and began free-lancing. He made *The Tall Men,* a successful western movie in 1955, *The King and Four Queens* (1956), *Band of Angels* (1957), *Teacher's Pet* (1958), *Run Silent, Run Deep* (1958), *But Not For Me* (1959), *It Started In Naples* (1960), and his last film, *The Misfits,* released in 1961.

He began work on *The Misfits* in July, 1960. It was filmed on location in Nevada and the work was hard and long. Co-stars Marilyn Monroe and Montgomery Clift were having personal problems, but Gable was his usual professional self. The emotional turmoil, as well as the physical effort of doing several of his own stunts took their toll. Clark Gable died of a heart attack a short time after the end of filming on November 16, 1960. He was fifty-nine years old. *Look* magazine did a cover story on the film

Window card for the movie *Teacher's Pet* made by Perlberg—Seaton Productions for Paramount. It was produced in 1958 and co-starred Clark Gable and Doris Day.

86

and the death of Gable on January 31, 1961. He did not live to see the birth of his only son who was also featured on a *Look* cover for August 29, 1961.

It has been sixty years since Gable began his movie career at M-G-M. He did not have roles in films which made statements or films that changed the world. Gable's films were made for entertainment: pure enjoyment. Because of their high entertainment value, Gable's best films are still fun to watch and new fans can have the pleasure of getting acquainted with the screen character (naughty but nice) that was Clark Gable.

For information on the Clark Gable Fan Club or the *Gone With the Wind Society* write:

Associated Graphics, Arts and Letters
Attention Cynthia Molt
364 North May Ave.
Monrovia, CA 91016

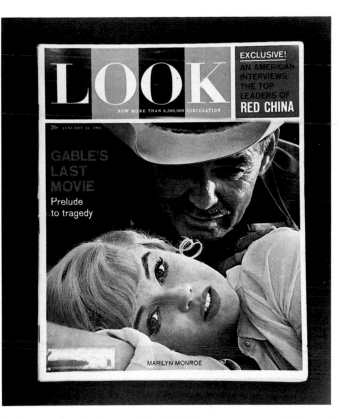

Look magazine for January 31, 1961 did a cover story on Gable and Marilyn Monroe and their last movie, *The Misfits* .

A lobby card from *The Misfits* made for United Artist Corporation in 1961. Shown are Gable and his co-star, Marilyn Monroe.

After Clark Gable's death, Look continued its coverage of "The King" with a cover story of his wife and his new son. The magazine is from August 29, 1961.

Many fan magazines featured cover pictures of Judy Garland including *Screen Album* for Fall, 1943.

Judy's hit song, "The Trolley Song" was from the 1944 M-G-M film, *Meet Me in St. Louis*. The words and music were by Hugh Martin and Ralph Blane. Leo Feist, Inc. published the music.

An advertisement for one of Judy Garland's non-musical films, *The Clock*, was featured in *Photoplay* magazine for May, 1945.

Photoplay for July, 1943 also used Judy for their cover material.

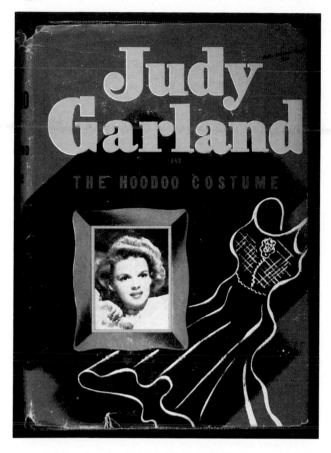

A book called *Judy Garland and the Hoodoo Costume* was published by the Whitman Publishing Co. in 1945. The book still has its dust jacket.

The M-G-M film, *The Harvey Girls* brought Judy another hit song in 1945 when she sang "On the Atchison, Topeka and the Santa Fe". The music was by Harry Warren and the lyrics were by Johnny Mercer. The music was published by Leo Feist, Inc.

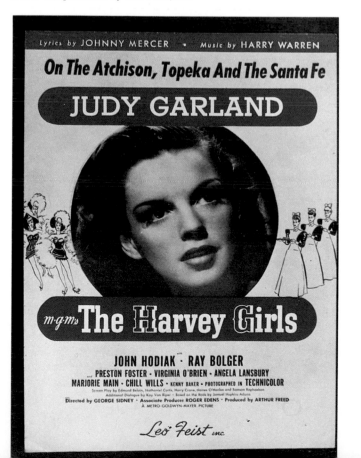

Screen Stories for May, 1948 carried an ad for the new M-G-M film. *The Pirate* starring Judy Garland and Gene Kelly.

over for Gene Kelly, because Kelly had broken his ankle. *Easter Parade* was in the top half-dozen grossing movies of the year.

After the completion of the musical, Judy made another suicide attempt and was hospitalized. Even though she was still not ready to resume work, the studio put her into *Annie Get Your Gun*. She tried to perform but was not doing well and was dropped from the film.

Later Joe Pasternak asked the studio heads for Judy to be allowed to star in a film which had been planned for June Allyson. Since June was pregnant, he needed a musical star to work with Van Johnson in the movie called *In the Good Old Summertime*. M-G-M gave him permission to use Judy and she turned in a fine performance.

Judy continued to be plagued by bad health and was hospitalized once more in 1949. Metro picked up the tab on her hospital stay but after several weeks she was told to go back to work or she would be released from her contract.

Judy returned to the studio where Joe Pasternak was producing another film called *Summer Stock*. He asked that Judy be allowed to star in it in spite of her shaky health. Judy's reputation for poor work habits intensified with the making of this movie. She was often late, and was generally very hard to work with.

After filming had wrapped, an additional musical number was needed and Judy was called in to do "Get Happy." The song turned out to be the high point of the picture even though Judy had lost a lot of weight since she had made the rest of the movie and the change in her appearance was quite obvious. The number was the last filming she would do for M-G-M. *Movie Story* magazine for November, 1950 carried pictures and the story from Judy's last M-G-M film.

A movie still of Judy Garland and Fred Astaire taken from their delightful M-G-M musical, *Easter Parade* from 1948.

Movie Story magazine for November, 1950 contains a story and pictures from Judy Garland's last film for M-G-M, *Summer Stock* made in 1950.

Only three weeks after she finished *Summer Stock*, the studio had attempted to put Judy in a new film called *Royal Wedding* with Fred Astaire. Judy began work on the movie but she wasn't able to continue. She was fired not only from the picture but also from the studio. It was 1950, she was twenty-eight years old and broke.

It is hard for the average person to understand how Judy Garland could have made millions of dollars during her career and yet spend the last twenty years of her life in debt. She had, of course, never learned to manage money. Her mother had apparently helped her spend her early earnings and her living expenses were always high. She employed several people for household help. Since Judy always considered herself a star she continued to live expensively even when the funds weren't available.

After her parting with M-G-M, Sid Luft and concerts came into her life. Luft became her promoter, manager and husband (June 11, 1952). Luft was also the father of Judy's other two children, Lorna, born in 1952 and Joseph, born in 1955. Judy Garland began her concert career in 1951 with a smash performance at the London Palladium. That fall she moved on to the Palace Theatre in New York. Her concerts were sold-out nightly. She played for nineteen weeks and did 184 performances before nearly 800,000 people. Judy Garland was back on top.

With her career now a viable asset, Judy and Luft decided to try to get her another movie role. He would produce the film and she would be the star. They settled on a musical remake of *A Star Is Born* for Warners. The film was completed with James Mason as her co-star. *Life* magazine again made Judy its cover girl for September 13, 1954 and the film was also featured in *Screen Stories* for August, 1954.

A window card from *In the Good Old Summertime*, the M-G-M film from 1949 which starred Judy Garland and Van Johnson.

A program from the Palace Theatre in New York for the week beginning October 22, 1951 when Judy brought her two-a-day act to the theatre, played for nineteen weeks and did 184 performances.

Judy gave one of her finest performances in the picture and was nominated for an Academy Award. She was still in the hospital after the birth of her son, Joey, at the time of the ceremony. People were so sure that she would win the award for best actress of 1954 that television cameras were set up in her hospital room to film her joyful reaction to the good news. When the announcement was made, she didn't win. The Oscar instead went to Grace Kelly for her role in *The Country Girl*. Most fans feel that decision was one of the greatest mistakes ever made by the Academy members. *A Star Is Born* did very well financially but because of its cost (estimates from $10 million and up) it did not make Judy a wealthy woman even though it was one of the year's top ten grossers.

During the next six years, Judy did cabaret and concert work, mostly under Luft's management. Their marriage was a stormy one and they separated in 1960. That same year Judy again played the London Palladium and on April 23, 1961 she made a triumphant return to the top when she gave a concert at Carnegie Hall. Her work that night has been called her greatest performance ever. Judy's two-record recording of the concert was also successful and sold over two million copies. After she finished singing the audience just seemed to gravitate to the footlights to try to communicate with Judy Garland. It was a very unusual happening because many people in the audience were stars themselves and they were just as swept away by emotion as Judy's lesser known fans.

A poster advertising Judy Garland's triumphant Carnegie Hall concert for April 23, 1961.

A Star is Born, the film which brought Judy Garland an Oscar nomination was featured in story and pictures in *Screen Stories* for August, 1954.

97

In 1945 Columbia produced another film for Rita that they hoped would be as good as *Cover Girl*. It was called *Tonight and Every Night*. It was not a great picture but it still made money. By this time, Rita was so famous she was receiving 6,000 fan letters each week.

As a result of her tremendous popularity, Rita was able to negotiate a new contract with Columbia in 1946 that would give her 25% of the profit from her films plus her salary. In the same year, she made a movie, called *Gilda*, that would establish forever Rita's image as "The Love Goddess." Rita as Gilda in the long black strapless gown and full-length gloves became as much a Rita trademark as her *Life* magazine pin-up pose wearing a lace nightgown. Her performance of the song, "Put the Blame on Mame" is a classic moment in film.

In 1947 *Life* magazine did its famous cover story on Rita called "The Love Goddess in America" in its November 10th issue. The article also mentioned her new movie called *Down to Earth* in which she played another "love goddess." Her income for the year was $375,000 and she was at the peak of her career.

In 1948 Orson and Rita joined forces to make a movie called *The Lady From Shanghai*. For the film, Wells insisted that Rita's long hair be cut and bleached blonde. Although Rita always had faith in the film, her public liked her better as a redhead and the movie did not do well at the box office. The end of the filming also marked the end of the Wells-Hayworth marriage and Rita immediately took a trip to Europe to rest and relax.

Modern Screen for March, 1944 featured Rita on the cover.

Sheet music from Columbia's hit Rita Hayworth movie, *Cover Girl* from 1944. The song was also a hit, "Long Ago (and Far Away)" by Jerome Kern and Ira Gershwin. It was published by Crawford Music Corp.

Photoplay for February, 1943 also used Rita Hayworth as cover art.

Screen Romance for February, 1945 contained an ad for Rita's successful film called *Tonight and Every Night*.

An advertisement for the Rita Hayworth—Columbia film called *Down to Earth* released in 1947.

One of Rita's most famous films—*Gilda*—was advertised in *Photoplay* magazine for April, 1946. The ad pictured Rita in her well known black strapless dress. Glenn Ford was Rita's co-star.

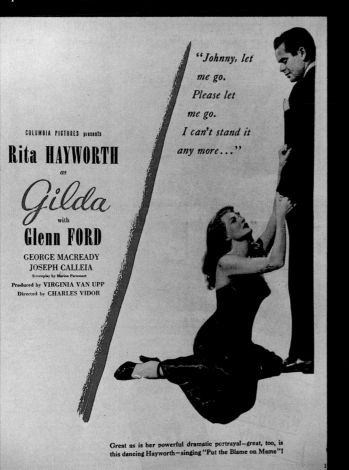

In Europe, Rita met Prince Aly Khan and they began a well publicized year-long courtship that crossed continents and oceans. Because they were both married to others at the beginning of their affair, the scandal could have damaged Rita's career. Surprisingly, Rita's popularity did not diminish.

In the middle of her romance she came back to the United States to make the film *The Loves of Carmen* again co-starring with Glen Ford (her *Gilda* co-star as well). Although the film wasn't well received, several products were produced to tie-in with the movie's release. Paper dolls were printed by Saalfield in 1948 (#1529 and #5161) to add to the movie's publicity. A 14″ tall composition doll of Rita in one of her Carmen costumes was also made at this time by the Uneeda Doll Co. Because the doll is not marked, it is difficult to identify. The doll's original tag read "The Carmen Doll Inspired by Rita Hayworth's Portrayal of Carmen in *The Loves of Carmen*."

By May of 1949 both the Prince and Rita had received divorces and the couple was married in the town hall of Vallauris near the Moslem Prince's home. Their daughter Yasmin was born in December of the same year. Although Rita was willing to give up her career for a domestic life with the Prince, he seemed more intent on continuing his "playboy" life style. Rita left Europe and Aly Khan in 1951 to return to the United States. Rita resumed her movie career at Columbia when she starred in *Affair in Trinidad* in 1952. In 1953 she made *Salome*. Both pictures were box office successes.

Even though Rita didn't make a movie from 1949-1951 she was not forgotten by her public. She was still included on the movie star calendar for the year of 1950.

A lobby card for Rita's movie made by Columbia called, *Affair in Trinidad*, which was produced after Rita left Prince Aly Khan in 1952

These paper dolls of Rita Hayworth were published by Saalfield Publishing Co. in 1948 as a tie-in to the movie, *The Loves of Carmen* made by Rita, for Columbia, in the same year.

This 15″ tall Rita Hayworth doll was made by the Uneeda Doll Co. in 1948. It is all-composition with a red mohair wig, sleep eyes, and a closed mouth. The doll is unmarked, but its original tag identified it as a "Carmen" doll inspired by Rita Hayworth's Carmen in the movie, *The Loves of Carmen*. She is all original wearing a red taffeta dress with a black mesh overskirt and mantilla, both trimmed with red flowers. She wears gold shoes and the bodice of the dress is trimmed in gold rickrack.

The movie program for, *Salome*, the Columbia film from 1953 that featured Rita Hayworth doing a highly publicized "Dance of the Seven Veils." Her co-star was Stewart Granger.

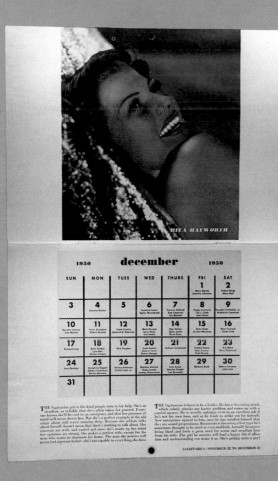

Window card for Rita's 1954 film, *Miss Sadie Thompson*, the movie based on Somerset Maugham's story *Rain*. Jose Ferrer was her co-star and the film was made by Columbia.

A movie star calendar for the year 1950 featured Rita's picture as the star for December. The calendar listed birthdays for all the biggest stars of the era. It was published by *Motion Picture* magazine.

After Rita's divorce from Aly Khan in 1953 she began keeping company with Dick Haymes. He had been a musical star in Twentieth Century-Fox Betty Grable musicals in the 1940s but was in financial and personal trouble when Rita befriended him in 1953. He was behind in income tax payments and was about to be deported to his native Argentina. Rita married him before the year was over. The marriage saved Haymes from deportation but he was still faced with money worries.

Rita's film for 1953 was *Miss Sadie Thompson* based on the W. Somerset Maugham story *Rain*. Although Rita got generally good reviews, the film was not successful.

Rita and Haymes separated in 1955 and she continued to fulfill her contract at Columbia. Rita made a now-forgotten movie called *Fire Down Below* in 1957. Also in 1957, Rita appeared in the last film she would ever make for Columbia, *Pal Joey*. The movie was based on the stage production of the same name. Kim Novak got the part that had originally been intended for Rita when the play was first purchased by Columbia years earlier, leaving Rita to play the "older woman." Frank Sinatra had the male lead.

When Rita's contract was over in 1957, she had been with Columbia Studios for twenty years. Her pictures helped make the company into a major studio. In total, *Cover Girl, Tonight and Every Night* and *Gilda* grossed $20,000,000 for the studio.

In 1958 Rita married her fifth and last husband, James Hill, a screenwriter and producer. Hill arranged for Rita to be cast in the award winning United Artists film, *Separate Tables* which was

Press book made for the United Artists film *Separate Tables* in 1958. Rita shared the billing with Deborah Kerr, David Niven and Wendy Hiller.

113

released the same year. Both Rita, the film, and the other cast members (Deborah Kerr, David Niven and Wendy Hiller) were praised highly and the picture was very successful.

Rita and Hill separated in 1961 but Hayworth continued to make films for many different studios (eleven movies in all). She made her last picture called *The Wrath of God* in 1972 for Metro-Goldwyn-Mayer.

Health and alcohol problems shadowed Rita's middle-age, and in 1976 a widely published picture of a disheveled Rita leaving a plane in London gave all her fans cause for concern. It wasn't until 1980 that Miss Hayworth was diagnosed as being the victim of Alzheimer's disease. Her daughter Yasmin became her guardian and moved Rita to New York where she could look after her. The two remained in close touch daily until Rita's death in 1987.

Because of her early death and poor health during her last years, a Rita Hayworth autograph has become rather scarce and, therefore, it is one of the more desirable star autographs for collectors.

Rita Hayworth's career as the "Love Goddess" only lasted about ten years. Yet, subsequent generations of moviegoers and movie-makers have been unable to find another star who could assume the title. It seems apparent that there will be only one "Love Goddess": Rita Hayworth.

Autographs of Rita Hayworth are highly collectible and fans lucky enough to own Miss Hayworth's signature are fortunate.

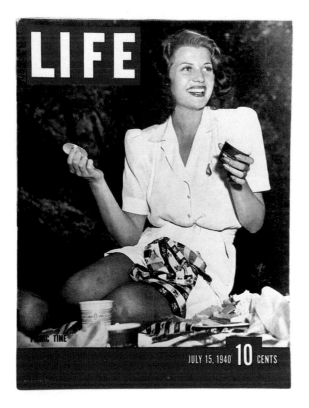

Rita Hayworth appeared on her first *Life* cover on July 15, 1940 before she became labeled as the "Love Goddess."

The lovely Rita will always be remembered as she looked in the cover photo on the sheet music "Dearly Beloved" from her Astaire-Columbia movie, *You Were Never Lovelier* from 1942. The music was by Jerome Kern and Johnny Mercer. It was published by Chappell in 1942.

Sonja Henie
Queen of the Ice

This commercial picture of Sonja Henie was given away by a movie theater to promote business for Sonja's films.

Sonja Henie made her way to the Hollywood screen in a very unique way, she traveled the road to fame and fortune on ice skates.

Born in Oslo, Norway in 1912, Sonja was the daughter of a well-to-do businessman. When she showed an interest in ice skating at the age of six, Sonja's father purchased her first pair of skates. She was soon spending five hours a day on the ice in order to compete in skating exhibitions. With her family's financial backing, she was able to travel to other countries for lessons and advice to improve her skating ability.

Sonja soon received world attention as a figure skater. At the age of fourteen she was declared the ice skating champion of Norway. In 1927, at the age of fifteen, she was awarded the world skating championship. Sonja was able to hold the world champion title for a total of ten years. In 1928 she won her first Olympic Gold Medal in figure skating. Sonja went on to win again in 1932

and 1936. Sonja continues to be the only person to achieve three consecutive ice skating championships in the Olympics.

As Sonja prepared for her Olympic contests, she decided to add choreography to the free-style skating part of her program so that she could combine dancing and skating. Sonja had taken dance lessons for many years and with the help of her family's financial resources, she was able to study ballet with the Russian ballerina, Karsavina. Sonja used what she had learned from Karsavina to change the look of free-style skating forever. Today's figure skaters continue to use some of the new dance-based moves Miss Henie brought to ice skating.

In 1936 Sonja announced she would turn professional after her final Olympics. She wanted to continue skating but she also needed to have an income so that she could begin to pay back some of the thousands of dollars her family had invested in her training and traveling during her amateur skating career. Her ultimate goal was to appear in movies but she was very particular about what kind of movies she wanted to make. She did not want to just skate in a specialty number in someone else's film. Sonja wanted to star in movies built around her and her skating. With the studio system still very much in place in the 1930s, each film company had their own stable of starlets being groomed for stardom. It was customary for these starlets to start out at the bottom in bit parts, work up to supporting, and then starring roles. It was very unusual for a producer to take a chance on an unknown in a leading part. Luckily, Sonja Henie was not just anyone, she had been the Olympic ice skating champion three times in a row.

After the 1936 Olympics Sonja and her father planned a skating tour to nine United States cities. The cities to be covered were all located in the East. The Henies were hoping that producers from Hollywood would come to watch Sonja skate. Although the tour was a sell-out, and people loved the exhibition, Hollywood offers were not forthcoming. Mr. Henie decided that since the producers had not come to them, they would go to the producers. He managed to find an ice rink in Los Angeles that could be rented for a few weeks and they took their show to California.

The plan worked. Several Hollywood producers attended the opening of the ice skating program and were interested in Miss Henie but not on her terms. Sonja was disappointed because the producer she really wanted to work with had not contacted her. He was Darryl Zanuck from Twentieth Century-Fox. Zanuck did come to see the show on the second night, expressed interest, and began negotiations with Sonja immediately. At first, he, like the others, only wanted to use her as a specialty act but, at last, Sonja convinced him that her idea would work and she signed a five year contract with Twentieth Century-Fox.

Sonja's first film called *One in a Million* was made in 1936. The movie co-starred Don Ameche and was based on the story of Sonja herself-an Olympic skater who turns professional and makes good. The film was a great box office success. Her 1937 film, *Thin Ice* (with Tyrone Power) was also a winner and Sonja was quickly ranked among the top ten stars of Hollywood, listed in eighth position.

In 1938 Sonja made two hit films: *Happy Landing* with Don Ameche and *My Lucky Star* with Richard Greene. Sonja's standing in the top ten moved up to number three with the success of these two movies.

Sonja Henie had always been known as a fine business woman, and as a result of this success, Sonja felt she was worth more money. She negotiated a new contract that would pay her $160,000 per film for three pictures a year. If she had really made three pictures a year, she would have been the highest paid star in Hollywood.

Sonja also began a new project in 1938. She had always wanted to perform in ice shows so ice skating could be publicized and popularized. She and a partner, Arthur Wirtz, began the Hollywood Ice Revue in 1938 and this show was to become an annual touring event. Sonja, herself, skated in the revue until 1952. Because of the scarcity of ice skaters in California, they took dancers and trained them to skate. Sonja was able to do what she had set out to do. Ice dancing caught on and several ice shows still make annual tours in different countries all over the world.

Even though Sonja Henie was not a child star, she did attract so much attention from the public as a skating movie star that products were made in the toy industry to take advantage of her fame.

Sonja's Twentieth Century-Fox film for 1937 was called *Thin Ice* and a picture of the two stars, Sonja and Tyrone Power, was on the cover of *The Family Circle* on October 1, 1937 to promote the new movie.

"A Gypsy Told Me" sheet music from Twentieth Century-Fox's 1938 film *Happy Landing*. The words and music are by Sam Pokrass and Jack Yellen. It was published by the Crawford Music Corp.

An advertisement for Sonja's first film made for Twentieth Century-Fox was featured in the *Screen Play* magazine for February, 1937. The title of the movie was *One in a Million*.

116

Sheet music from the Twentieth Century-Fox film *My Lucky Star* from 1938 in which Richard Greene starred with Sonja. The song "I've Got a Date With a Dream" was written by Mack Gordon and Harry Revel. The song was published by Leo Feist, Inc.

This Sonja Henie *Hollywood Ice Revue* program is for the 1940-1941 touring season. Sonja Henie was featured as the star.

The European program for the 1947 *Hollywood Ice Revue* which also starred Sonja Henie.

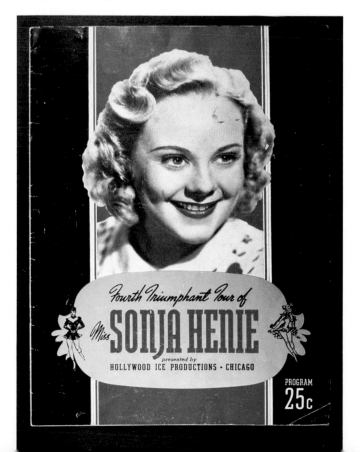

The Madame Alexander Doll Co. made an all-composition Sonja Henie doll complete with ice skates beginning in 1939. About the only similarity between the doll and Sonja were the doll's dimples modeled after the famous star's. It came in sizes of 14", 18", and 21". The doll is very collectible, especially when in excellent condition and dressed in original clothing. The doll was such a success that the Alexander Co. continued to make it for several years.

The first Sonja Henie paper dolls were also produced in 1939. This lovely set had three dolls plus copies of the costumes from Miss Henie's movies. It was published by Merrill Publishing Co. and is #3475. These are the nicest of the several sets of Sonja paper dolls.

The Merrill company also brought out a Sonja Henie coloring book the same year. It is #3476 and the pictures to color told the story of Sonja's life. Another coloring book was published by the same firm in 1940 called *Sonja Henie; Paint Her Pictures* #3491.

Miss Henie's first movie for 1939 was called *Second Fiddle* and she again co-starred with Tyrone Power. Most of these films took place in a winter resort and the plots were usually "boy gets girl, boy loses girl, boy gets girl", but they were entertaining movies and the fans loved to see Sonja skate. Her second film for 1939 was *Everything Happens at Night* with a new co-star, Ray Milland.

As Sonja's fame grew, so did people's interest in her as a screen personality. Even national magazines did features on the new skating star. *Time* did a cover story on Sonja in their July 17, 1939 issue and *Look* magazine featured her on its cover on February 1, 1938. Publicity photos were also distributed to fans by Fox to promote Sonja's screen career. They were probably used as give aways at movie theaters to promote an upcoming Sonja film. These photographs are especially attractive when matted with an original Sonja Henie autograph. These autographs are still reasonably priced.

Though a little chubby in 1936 and 1937, Miss Henie lost weight in the late 1930s and remained slim through the rest of her career. She was never without exercise and was a fine swimmer, skier, and tennis player in addition to her skating.

In 1940, Merrill published another set of Sonja Henie paper dolls, #3492. The book contains three dolls but the quality is not quite as good as the earlier dolls from 1939. The last set of Sonja Henie paper dolls was produced in 1941 and are #3418.

Sonja Henie added writing to her talents when she became an author in 1940. Her autobiography, called *Wings On My Feet*, was published by Prentice-Hall. The book contains pictures of her early career and also provides instructions on how to do some of Sonja's skating moves.

These Sonja Henie paper dolls were published by the Merrill Publishing Co. in 1939. The book contains three different dolls and clothing based on Sonja's movie costumes. The number of the book is #3475.

This 14″ tall Sonja Henie doll was made by the Madame Alexander Doll Co. in 1939. The doll is all-composition with sleep eyes, open mouth, and wig. She is marked on the back of her head "Madame Alexander Sonja Henie." The doll is wearing her original clothing.

This Sonja Henie coloring book #3476 was published by the Merrill Publishing Co. in 1939. The pictures to color tell the story of Sonja's life.

118

The sheet music "I'm Sorry For Myself" from Twentieth Century-Fox's movie called *Second Fiddle* from 1939. The music is by Irving Berlin and was published by Irving Berlin Inc. in 1939.

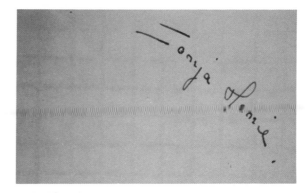

This Sonja Henie autograph was secured by an admirer years ago and is still very collectible.

These Sonja Henie paper dolls #3492 were published by Merrill in 1940. This set is rather faded in color and does not have the quality of the other Merrill products. There are three paper dolls in the set.

Look magazine did a cover story on Sonja Henie in their February 1, 1938 issue. The inside article was called, "Why Sonja Henie Left Home."

Sonja Henie's autobiography was published by Prentice-Hall in 1940. It is called *Wings On My Feet*.

Nicer Sonja Henie paper dolls numbered 3418 were published by Merrill in 1941. This was the final paper doll book in the series. The set contains two dolls and clothing.

By 1939, Sonja Henie was still in the list of the top ten Hollywood stars but had fallen to number ten. Her films were still successful, however, and in 1941 she made another skating movie called *Sun Valley Serenade*. John Payne was her co-star. The film also featured Glenn Miller and his orchestra, and his hit song, "Chattanooga Choo Choo."

During the early years of World War II when most fan magazines were focusing on the pin up girls-Betty Grable, Lana Turner and Rita Hayworth-Sonja continued to get her share of coverage. Today, fans particularly enjoy the magazines which feature her on the cover.

The Twentieth Century-Fox *Iceland* film for 1942 again starred Sonja with John Payne. It was a typical movie from the era featuring the U.S. Marines, lots of military uniforms and patriotism.

Sonja made one more movie for Twentieth Century-Fox in 1943. The picture called *Wintertime* was not as successful as the earlier films. With the novelty of a skating movie star wearing off, Sonja's contract was not renewed.

Even though Sonja was through at Fox, she signed with International to do a film called *It's a Pleasure* in 1945 with Michael O'Shea. In 1948 Sonja made *The Countess of Monte Carlo* for Universal. The movie was such a flop that Sonja retired from films.

After two unsuccessful marriages, to Dan Topping in 1940 and to Winthrop Gardiner in 1949, Sonja married a childhood sweetheart, Neils Onstad in 1956. They were still married at the time of her death in 1969 at the age of 57. Sonja died from leukemia as she was being flown home to Norway in an ambulance plane.

Sonja Henie accomplished a lot during her film career. She had invented the ice musical and made eleven films in twelve years which grossed a total of $25 million. At her death, she was one of the ten richest women in the world.

The "Chattanooga Choo Choo" was made famous by Glenn Miller and was also featured in the Twentieth Century-Fox movie for 1941 called *Sun Valley Serenade* with Sonja and John Payne. The music is by Harry Warren and the lyrics are by Mack Gordon. It was published by Leo Feist Inc.

Sonja was a favorite cover girl for the movie magazines of the period. She is pictured on the *Modern Screen* cover for March, 1942.

Although Sonja Henie never became a very good actress, she did what she set out to do-she publicized and popularized ice skating. Her innovative ice shows still prosper and the entertainment they provide the _____ makes a fitting memorial to the young Olympic star fr...

Sonja's Twentieth Century-Fox movie *Wintertime* received a full page ad in *Movie Stars Parade* for September, 1943.

Big Star Album No. 2 from 1943 also featured Sonja Henie as its cover art.

Pictured is a lobby card from 1942 for the Twentieth Century-Fox movie, *Iceland,* showing stars Sonja Henie, Jack Oakie, and John Payne.

Baby Sandy
Alias Sandra Lee Henville

This studio postcard of Baby Sandy was sent to a fan in August, 1941.

The name Sandra Lee Henville may not be familiar to most movie fans but doll and paper doll collectors all know Sandra's screen personality, Baby Sandy, because of the many products that were produced in the young star's image during her short career. Sandy began appearing in movies when she was little more than a year old and her career was over by the time she was four.

Movie stardom happened so early in Baby Sandy's life that grown-up Sandra Lee Henville doesn't even remember her years in the spotlight. Even though Baby Sandy made eight films and worked with stars as big as Bing Crosby, Sandra spent most of her adult working years as a legal secretary in Los Angeles.

Sandy's first appearance before a movie camera seems purely a result of luck and coincidence. In 1938, Sandra's father, Roy Henville, was a milkman in the Los Angeles area. He had read a story in the newspaper that Universal Studios needed a ten month old baby for a role in a new Bing Crosby picture. The Henvilles had a year-old daughter named Sandra, that they thought was pretty special. They were shy about trying to get the part for Sandra so Mr. Henville left some snapshots of his daughter on the doorstep at Charles Previn's home (music director at Universal) along with the milk. Mr. Previn took the pictures to work and showed them to the director of the movie, David Butler. Mr. Butler was sufficiently impressed and cast the child in the film. The movie baby was supposed to be a boy, but Sandra was already working on the picture before the error was discovered. The studio changed her name to Sandy and continued to pretend she was a boy, although the secret was not kept for long.

The movie was called *East Side of Heaven* and Sandy's co-star was Bing Crosby. With the success of Sandy's first film in 1939, more movies were lined up for Universal's tiny star.

The sheet music "Sing a Song of Sunbeams" from the Universal Pictures movie, *East Side of Heaven*. The music is by James Monaco and the lyrics are by Johnny Burke. It was published by Santly-Joy-Select, Inc. in 1939.

A new picture, *Unexpected Father* was written just for Sandy and it, too, was released in 1939. Hugh Herbert and Anne Gwynne played with Sandy in the film. Because of the immediate popularity of the tiny tot, her name was already being displayed above the title of the film in the movie posters.

The studio managed to get one more picture finished in 1939, a film called *Little Accident* which included Mischa Auer in the cast along with Dennis O'Keefe and Shirley Ross.

The products that were made to take advantage of the baby's fame began to appear in the same year. The 1930s were a bonanza for collectors of personality dolls. Shirley Temple, the Dionne Quintuplets, Jane Withers, Judy Garland, Deanna Durbin and England's Princess Elizabeth had all been modeled in doll form. Baby Sandy was another prime candidate to join the doll parade and Freundlich Novelty Corp. purchased the rights to make the doll in 1939. The dolls were on the market that same year and continued to be made until 1942 when Baby Sandy was a baby no longer. The dolls came in sizes of 8″, 12″, 15″, and 19″. The smaller dolls have painted eyes while the larger dolls have sleep eyes. The dolls are toddler models made of all-composition with molded hair emphasizing Sandy's trademark curl on her forehead.

Even *Life* magazine took note of the rising young star when Sandy became their cover girl at the age of eighteen months. The picture story inside the magazine described how Baby Sandy had been discovered.

An 8″ tall all-composition Baby Sandy doll in near mint condition. The doll is all original, complete with her Baby Sandy button. She has painted eyes, molded hair, and jointed limbs. She is marked on the back of the head, "Baby Sandy." The doll was made by the Freundlich Novelty Corp. from 1939-1942.

One sheet movie poster from the Baby Sandy Universal Pictures movie called *Unexpected Father* from 1939.

A 12″ tall model of the Baby Sandy doll with sleep eyes and open mouth with teeth was also made. This doll has been redressed in a copy of the original romper outfit.

The original pin that came on the Baby Sandy dolls is pictured here.

This is the largest of the Baby Sandy dolls which is 19′ tall. All three dolls were made by the Freundlich Corp. and all are marked "Baby Sandy" on the back of the heads. This doll is wearing a commercial outfit from the 1940s.

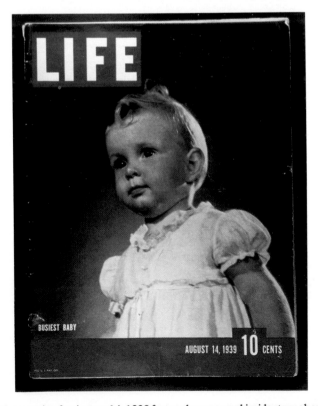

Life magazine for August 14, 1939 featured a cover and inside story about Baby Sandy.

Universal Pictures continued their work with Sandy in 1940 when two films were made: *Sandy is a Lady* with Nan Grey and Mischa Auer and *Sandy Gets Her Man* with Stuart Erwin and Una Merkel.

As Sandy's popularity continued, more products were added to the Baby Sandy line. Storybooks, pull toys, coloring books, drinking mugs, paper dolls, and even diapers were endorsed with Sandy's name.

Two sets of Baby Sandy paper dolls were issued, and both are highly prized by collectors. The first set was made by Whitman in 1940 and is numbered 996. The book had one large Baby Sandy doll and clothing drawn by the famous paper doll artist, Queen Holden. A copy of this set was printed as an advertising premium by Lysol Disinfectant. The second set was by the Merrill Publishing Co. #3426 and came out in 1941.

A book telling the story of Baby Sandy was also published in 1939. It was produced by Rand McNally and was full of pictures of the young star.

A metal cup made by Perco and marked on the bottom, "Baby Sandy's Cup" was probably another advertising premium used to promote the tiny movie actress. The cup itself, appears to be made of aluminum.

Although Sandy was growing up, Universal continued to publicize her as Baby Sandy and they put her in two more movies in 1941. She was in a studio musical called *Melody Lane* with

A one sheet movie poster from Baby Sandy's Universal film, *Sandy Gets Her Man* made in 1940.

One sheet movie poster from Baby Sandy's Universal film, *Sandy is a Lady* which was made in 1940.

A booklet called *Baby Sandy's Health Charts*. It was used as a premium by Lysol Disinfectants and contained health information for a new baby as well as pictures of Baby Sandy. It also included a copy of the earlier paper doll by Queen Holden with clothing to cut out.

125

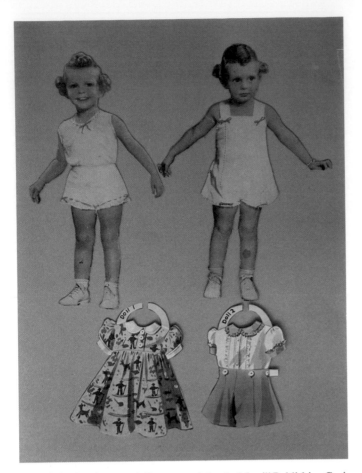

A metal cup marked on the bottom, "Baby Sandy's Cup" made by Perco. It may have been an advertising premium for a company to tie-in with Baby Sandy's movie fame.

These Baby Sandy paper dolls were made by the Merrill Publishing Co. in 1941 and were #3426. The set has two Baby Sandy dolls and clothes.

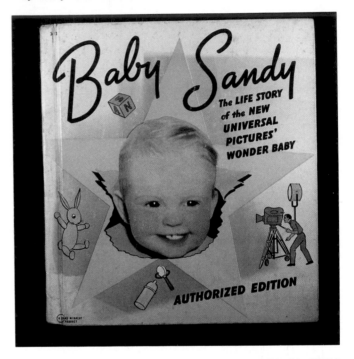

A book called *The Life Story of Baby Sandy* was published in 1939 by Rand McNally and Co. It is full of pictures of the young star.

Scrapbook pages from the 1930s featuring pictures from Sandy's movie days.

Anne Gwynne and Robert Paige and in her last film for Universal, *Bachelor Daddy* with Edward Everett Horton.

As Sandy passed the toddler age and became a four year old child, the name she had used to gain fame, Baby Sandy, no longer applied and Universal Pictures did not continue to use her in films. Sandy made her last picture for Republic Pictures in 1942. She played in *Johnny Doughboy* with another child star trying to make a transition to older roles, Jane Withers.

Sandy's film career was over in 1942, but there are still many fans who remember her. Sandy's fame came not so much from her films, which are rarely seen today, but through the products she endorsed, the fan magazines from the era, and through pictures in scrapbooks from her early years. By the time Sandy was four, she had outgrown her baby cuteness. Although she was still a nice looking little girl, she didn't have the appeal or the talent of a Shirley Temple and there was no longer a place for her in the movies.

With the end of her movie career, Sandra Lee Henville's life returned to normal. She stayed in California where she attended South Pasadena High School and Pasadena City College. Sandra has been married twice and has three sons. Miss Henville ultimately made a place for herself in the business world instead of the film world by pursuing a career as a legal secretary in the office of the County Counsel in Los Angeles.

Although, by Hollywood standards, eight films might not be considered a major screen career, these four years of Baby Sandy mania produced a surprising number of collectibles which continue to keep the memory of Baby Sandra Henville alive.

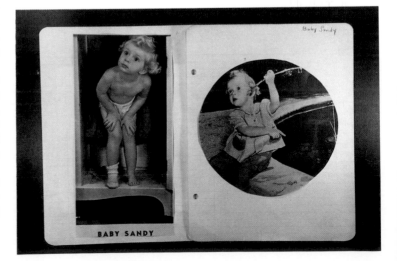

Al Jolson
The Jazz Singer

This autographed picture was sent out by Al Jolson's studio during his early film career.

Al Jolson, like Judy Garland, had a great rapport with a live audience. He seemed to thrive on the applause his performance evoked and he had a life-long reputation for putting on a show wherever he could assemble an audience. Jolson was a star entertainer in vaudeville, the theater, motion pictures, and on the radio. He had been a performer for nearly fifty years when he died in 1950.

Jolson was born Asa Yoelson in Russia in 1886 and came to America with his parents when he was only seven years old. The family settled in Washington D. C. where Mr. Yoelson became a cantor in the synagogue. He hoped his son would follow in his footsteps and also become a cantor, but young Asa had different ideas concerning his future. The boy was attracted to show

business at an early age and kept running away from home with the circus or the minstrel shows. Although Asa was always sent home, he continued to aspire to a "show biz" career.

Al Jolson made his first legitimate theater appearance in 1899 as one of a score of players in a mob scene in a play. This was followed by parts in minstrel shows and by 1909 he had worked his way up to the "end man" with the Lew Dockstader's Minstrels at $75 per week. When Al donned blackface to pinch hit for a missing star he was such a success he was picked to be in a Shubert production in the Winter Garden Theater in New York. The year was 1911 and the play was called *La Belle Paree* and Jolson (he had changed his name to Al Jolson) was a hit. For the next fourteen years, he was in New York appearing in hit musicals. Mostly he played a black-faced character called Gus. Sheet music from these productions is still available to collectors today for a reasonable price. Musicals included *Robinson Crusoe Jr.* in 1916, *Sinbad* in 1918, and *Bombo* in 1921.

Jolson's style of singing looks old-fashioned today. He was very emotional and often spoke some of the words from a kneeling position on the stage. He used black-face almost exclusively.

With Jolson's soaring popularity, he was coaxed into making a silent movie. Al was so dismayed when he saw the rushes that he wouldn't finish the picture. Things changed with the coming of sound.

In 1927, Warner Brothers planned to use a new talking device to make a movie that was part sound and part silent. The name of the film was *The Jazz Singer*. George Jessel had played the part on Broadway but negotiations couldn't be worked out between him and Warner Brothers, so the studio turned to Al Jolson. The sound was to be recorded on a disk that would be synchronized with the action. Most of the sound would be background music but Jolson would sing some songs and say a little dialogue. He was paid $75,000 to make the epic film. The story was very much like Jolson's own. It was about a boy whose father wanted him to become a cantor who, instead, becomes a famous popular singer. The movie was very favorably received and patrons were fascinated with the new "talkie." There weren't many theaters that had converted to sound so it was impossible for most people to view the new experimental movie. Fans, today, can still see the "first talkie" on video cassette.

By the time the next Jolson musical movie was ready in 1928, more theaters had sound equipment and *The Singing Fool* became one of the biggest of hits. It grossed over five million dollars and it held the record for most receipts until *Gone With the Wind* beat it in 1939. The hit song from the movie was *Sonny Boy*. The record Jolson made of "Sonny Boy" sold over a million copies.

Jolson sheet music is very collectible. This piece is from his hit show at the Winter Garden in 1916. The song is "Where the Black-eyed Susans Grow" by Dave Radford and Richard Whiting. The show was *Robinson Crusoe Jr.*. The music was published by Jerome M. Remick and Co. in 1917.

Sheet music from the show *Sinbad* from 1918 which starred Al Jolson. The song is one of Jolson's most famous, "My Mammy," by Joe Young, Sam Lewis, and Walter Donaldson. It was published by Irving Berlin, Inc. in 1921.

"California Here I Come" sheet music is from the Jolson hit show, *Bombo* from 1921. The music is by Jolson, B. G. de Sylva, and Joseph Meyer. It was published by M. Witmark and Sons.

An ad for Jolson's second movie, *The Singing Fool* made by Warners in 1928.

The program for the Al Jolson Warner Brothers picture from 1929 called *Say It With Songs*. The publication also has a section on the new Vitaphone sound process plus many pictures of Jolson and other Warner stars.

This 78 RPM record was recorded by Al Jolson from the movie, *The Singing Fool*. The song is "Sonny Boy" which sold over one million copies. The song was by Jolson, B. G. de Sylva, Lew Brown, and Ray Henderson. It was produced by Brunswick.

With the success he was having in the motion pictures, Al abandoned Broadway for a few years and concentrated on making movies. He was paid half a million dollars for each film. In 1929 he made another Warner Brothers film called *Say It With Songs*. *Screen Book* magazine covered the story of the film in its November, 1929 issue.

In 1930 Jolson's new movie was called *Mammy* and included the song, "Let Me Sing and I"m Happy." Lois Moran was his co-star.

By 1931 Jolson's films were not doing as well as his first efforts so he took a break and returned to Broadway to do *Wonder Bar*. The show was later made into a motion picture in 1932 with Jolson, Kay Francis and Dick Powell.

In 1932 Jolson added radio to his repertoire. Jolson continued to be a participant in radio broadcasts for the rest of his life, usually appearing as a guest on someone else's show.

In 1933, he returned to Hollywood to work for United Artists in a film called *Hallelujah I'm a Bum*. Although most critics believed it to be Jolson's best film up to that time, audiences apparently did not agree, and the film was not successful. Jolson was still considered to be one of the most famous of the Hollywood stars and he was included in the *Hollywood Movie Bingo Game* published by Whitman in 1937.

Al Jolson was married four times during his lifetime: to Henrietta Keller in 1906, to Alma Osborne in 1922, to Erle Galbraith in 1945 and to his most famous wife, Ruby Keeler in 1928. Their marriage lasted around ten years (they were divorced in 1939) and they adopted a son, Al Jolson Junior, in 1935.

The sheet music of "Let Me Sing and I'm Happy" from the Warner movie *Mammy* starring Al Jolson. The music is by Irving Berlin and it was published by Irving Berlin, Inc. in 1929.

Hollywood Movie Bingo: The Game of the Movie Stars was manufactured by the Whitman Publishing Co. in 1937. All the big Hollywood stars were represented including Jolson, Garbo, Chaplin, Cagney, Hepburn, Gable, Astaire, Crosby, Lombard, Tracy, and many more.

Sheet music from the Jolson film *Wonder Bar* made by First National in 1932. The film co-starred Kay Francis and Dick Powell. The song was called "Goin' to Heaven on a Mule" by Al Dubin and Harry Warren. The music was published by M. Witmark and Sons in 1934.

Jolson's wife, Ruby Keeler was featured as a paper doll in the *Chicago Sunday Tribune* Fashion Parade Series on December 13, 1936.

By 1935, Ruby Keeler had become a more famous film star than her husband. She had gained popularity as a dancer (rather heavy footed but attractive) and First National put them both in a film called *Go Into Your Dance*. The film is not really memorable except for the uniqueness of having the famous husband and wife in the same movie.

After several more undistinguished pictures, Jolson made a triumphant return to Broadway in 1940 in *Hold On To Your Hats*. He also took the show on the road after it closed in New York. Shortly after this success, World War II began and Al Jolson became a relentless entertainer for the troops on every war front. He sang his songs from the old days and gained new fans, in spite of the fact that most critics considered his style of entertainment outdated and old-fashioned. Jolson usually traveled for the USO, but he also did many shows independently, using his own money.

Jolson was so successful with the servicemen that Columbia decided to take a chance on making a movie of his life. Many screen biographies were made during the 1940s including James Cagney's big hit *Yankee Doodle Dandy*, the biography of George M. Cohan which was produced in 1942.

The film was to star a newcomer named Larry Parks playing Jolson and Jolson, himself, was to do the sound track for the songs. The film, called *The Jolson Story*, was released in 1946. It was amazingly successful and made a whole new career possible for Al Jolson. The screen play was featured in *Screen Romances* for November, 1946. Sheet music of the old songs were hot items again and best of all, Jolson's new recordings for the movie became hit records. The film became the fourth highest box office hit of the whole decade (grossing $13,000,000) and at his death, Jolson had received over $95,000 in royalties from the film.

This still is from *Go Into Your Dance* the movie made by First National which starred Jolson and his wife, Ruby Keeler. Pictured with Jolson is Patsy Kelly.

A book was published by the Saalfield Publishing Co. in 1935 to tie-in with the *Go Into Your Dance* movie. It features the story and scenes from the First National Production Corporation Picture.

Jolson returned to Broadway for a show called *Hold On To Your Hats*. This program is from the road company production which appeared in Chicago at the Grand Opera House in July, 1940.

Screen Romances magazine for November, 1946 featured pictures and the story of the movie, *The Jolson Story,* made by Columbia that gave the Jolson career a new life. Pictured are Larry Parks and Evelyn Keyes who played leading roles in the film.

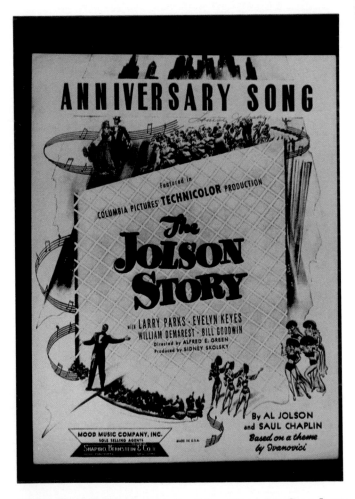

This 78 rpm record album was produced by Decca Records and featured the music from *The Jolson Story*. Jolson recorded the songs.

Columbia knew a good thing when they had it, so they did a sequel film in 1949 called *Jolson Sings Again* to bring the story up-to-date. Again records and sheet music sales climbed up the charts. Memorabilia from these two popular Jolson films can still be found by today's collectors at reasonable prices. Jolson even became a magazine cover subject once more when his photo was on the *Song Hits* magazine.

In 1950, during the Korean War, Jolson felt the pull of an audience once again and he volunteered to entertain the troops. He was 64 years old and had been in the entertainment business for nearly fifty years but he was always happiest when performing for an audience. He returned to the United States after a successful tour and suffered a heart attack in a San Francisco hotel. He died on October 23, 1950. The "Jazz Singer" was silenced at last.

Sheet music of the "Anniversary Song" from *The Jolson Story*. It was written by Al Jolson and Saul Chaplin. Larry Parks played the Jolson part in the hit film. The music was published by Mood Music, Inc.

Al Jolson left an estate of over two million dollars. He and the entertainment industry had been good for each other. In vaudeville, theater, movies, and radio Jolson had found his calling-an audience. "You ain't seen nothin' yet" he would say and his public relaxed as they settled into their theater seats for another happy half hour of Jolson's songs.

For Interested Fans:

International Al Jolson Society, Inc.
2981 Westmoor Dr.
Columbus, OH 43204

Newsletters three or four times yearly
Convention and another publication annually $10 per year

Song Hits magazine for June, 1948 featured Al Jolson on its cover because of the new interest in the veteran performer.

Sheet music by Jolson was again popular in the late 1940s. This song, "Toot Toot, Tootsie" is by Gus Kahn, Ernie Erdman and Dan Russo. It was used in the film *Jolson Sings Again* and the music was published by Leo Feist, Inc. in 1949.

A new record album was produced by Decca in 1949 when Columbia made a sequel to the earlier hit movie. The new film was called, *Jolson Sings Again*. These records are 45 rpm.

Jeanette MacDonald
(With Nelson Eddy)

Jeanette MacDonald in a publicity photo released by her studio, Metro-Goldwyn-Mayer.

Operetta star Jeanette MacDonald's fifteen year film career ended forty years ago. Nevertheless, she is fondly remembered by many fans today as their favorite screen personality. As a result, collectibles from her screen career are very much in demand.

Jeanette MacDonald's screen biography lists her birth date as 1907 but her early school records recorded 1903 as her birth year. Jeanette was raised in Philadelphia, one of three daughters of Daniel and Anne MacDonald. Jeanette's father was a Philadelphia contractor until the family moved to New York where the girls began stage careers. Jeanette took singing and dancing lessons when she was a young girl and made her first local professional appearance in Philadelphia at the age of nine.

Jeanette joined her sister, Blossom, in the chorus at the Capitol Theater in New York City around 1920. By 1923 she had worked up to a leading role in the stage musical *The Magic Ring*. For the next four years, she played major roles in *Tip Top* in 1925, *Bubbling Over* in 1926, and in *Angela* in 1928. While in Chicago starring in *Boom*, Jeanette was seen by the Hollywood movie director, Ernst Lubitsch. Lubitsch cast her in the first original movie operetta opposite the famous French star, Maurice Chevalier. The film was called *The Love Parade* and was released in 1929 to great acclaim for its two stars. Jeanette continued her film career at Paramount in 1930 by making *The Vagabond King*, *Monte Carlo* and *Let's Go Native*.

In 1930, Jeanette was in a film for United Artists called *The Lottery Bride.* She continued her film career in 1931, making several movies for Fox including *Oh For a Man, Don't Bet On Women,* and *Annabelle's Affairs.* She developed into a fine light comedian as well as a singing star through these films.

Sheet music from an early MacDonald Paramount picture, *The Vagabond King* made in 1930. The song is "Only a Rose" by Brian Hooker and Rudolf Friml. It was published by Famous Music Corp.

In 1932, Jeanette was re-teamed with Chevalier at Paramount for *One Hour With You* and *Love Me Tonight*. Both films were successful and MacDonald's career was on the rise. The musicals MacDonald made at Paramount with Maurice Chevalier are considered by many movie critics to include some of her best film work. Unfortunately, it is hard for fans to locate these movies to see them today. In 1933 Jeanette signed a film contract at M-G-M and her first picture for the studio was *The Cat and the Fiddle* made in 1934. The movie was based on the Jerome Kern-Oscar Hammerstein operetta.

Jeanette made her final film with Chevalier in 1934 when they did the popular operetta, *The Merry Widow* for Metro-Goldwyn-Mayer. With the backing of M-G-M and because she became Metro head Louis B. Mayer's favorite star, MacDonald's film career was now moving into its best years. In 1935, the studio teamed its famous soprano with a newcomer to produce a Victor Herbert operetta called *Naughty Marietta*. The newcomer's name was Nelson Eddy and the pairing clicked. The film won an Academy Award for the best sound recording for 1935. *Popular Songs* magazine featured a beautiful redheaded Jeanette MacDonald on its February, 1935 cover. The success of Jeanette MacDonald and her screen partner, Nelson Eddy, continued to grow. In 1936, their new movie, *Rose Marie* was again received with tremendous satisfaction by their public and it is considered to be one of the best films the couple made. "Indian Love Call" is probably the song best remembered from the film. Just as Fred Astaire and Ginger Rogers became the most famous screen dance team, MacDonald and Eddy, "America's Sweethearts", became the best known of the screen's singing duos.

"One Hour With You" sheet music from the Paramount film called *One Hour With You* starring Maurice Chevalier with Jeanette MacDonald. Although Jeanette's picture is on the cover, her name is not mentioned. The song is by Leo Robin and Richard Whiting. The publisher was Famous Music Corp.

The *Romantic Movie Stories* magazine for April, 1935 did a cover story on the first MacDonald—Eddy film called *Naughty Marietta* made by Metro-Goldwyn-Mayer in 1935.

The *Popular Songs* magazine for February, 1935 featured Jeanette MacDonald on its cover.

An ad for the hit M-G-M movie, *San Francisco* starring Clark Gable and Jeanette MacDonald appeared in the *Photoplay* magazine for June, 1936.

"Rose Marie" sheet music from the M-G-M movie, *Rose Marie* from 1936. The lyrics are by Otto Harbach and Oscar Hammerstein, and the music is by Rudolf Friml. It was published by Harms. Jeanette MacDonald co-starred with Nelson Eddy in the film.

This "Will You Remember?" sheet music is from the M-G-M movie *Maytime* from 1937. The lyrics are by Rida Johnson Young and the music is by Sigmund Romberg. G. Schirmer, Inc. published the music. MacDonald and Eddy starred in the film.

MacDonald was ranked ninth on the Hollywood top ten list of stars in 1936. Her success continued even without Eddy as a partner when she made the hit movie, *San Francisco* with the "King" himself, Clark Gable. The movie was the story of the San Francisco earthquake and Jeanette's hit song from the film was "San Francisco."

By 1937 the yearly movies made by M-G-M starring "America's Sweethearts" were sure hits and 1937's *Maytime* was no exception. Some critics consider *Maytime* to be the best of their musicals together and this movie is said to be Jeanette's favorite, as well. Many of the MacDonald-Eddy films, including *Maytime*, are preserved on video tape and can be purchased through mail order catalogs.

Nineteen thirty-seven also became an important year in Jeanette's personal life when she married Gene Raymond, her husband until her death in 1965. MacDonald's other movie from 1937, *The Firefly* with Allan Jones was also successful; however the public continued to prefer her with co-star Nelson Eddy. Possibly to remedy the situation, two Eddy-MacDonald movies were released in 1938: *Girl of the Golden West* and *Sweethearts*. *Sweethearts* was the first all-color movie made by M-G-M and it was one of the top money makers for 1938. The fan magazines were still giving the two stars full coverage both in their personal lives and in their careers.

Sheet music "Giannina Mia" from the M-G-M MacDonald film from 1937 which co-starred Allan Jones. The music was by Rudolf Friml. The lyrics were by Otto A. Harbach. The movie was called *The Firefly*. G. Schirmer, Inc. was the music publisher.

Sheet music for the title M-G-M song from the MacDonald—Eddy film, *Sweethearts* from 1938. The song was by Victor Herbert, Bob Wright, and Chet Forrest. G. Schirmer, Inc. was the music publisher.

An advertisement for the movie, *Girl of the Golden West* from M-G-M appeared in the *Modern Screen* magazine for April, 1938.

Modern Movies for June, 1938 devoted its cover to Jeanette MacDonald.

Jeanette was the cover girl for *Modern Screen* in January, 1940.

The *Song Hits* magazine for August 1940 featured songs and pictures from the M-G-M MacDonald—Eddy film of that year called, *New Moon*.

Since two MacDonald-Eddy movies had been released in 1938, Jeanette did not co-star with Nelson Eddy in 1939. However, she did star in a forgettable Lew Ayres movie called *Broadway Serenade*.

In 1940 two more of the MacDonald-Eddy movies were released, *New Moon* and *Bitter Sweet*. *New Moon* had a Sigmund Romberg-Oscar Hammerstein score while *Bitter Sweet* was based on a Noel Coward show. Although some critics prefer these two movies over the MacDonald-Eddy films of 1938, by 1940 the public's interest in operettas was waning and the films are seldom heard of today. M-G-M still thought enough of Jeanette in 1940 to extend her contract for two more years.

In 1941 Jeanétte made no Eddy film, but starred with her husband, Gene Raymond, in the only movie they made together, *Smilin' Through*. During this same year Miss MacDonald was featured in a paper doll book published by Merrill Publishing Co. The book called, *Jeanette MacDonald Glorious Singing Star* is a favorite of paper doll collectors as well as movie buffs. The book features many of the costumes Miss MacDonald wore in her films. Since most of her pictures were period pieces, the costumes were always very elaborate and this book does them justice.

Merrill also produced a coloring book of MacDonald called *Jeanette MacDonald Costume Parade* in 1941. The book also contained a paper doll to color and cut out. This book, too, is much in demand by collectors.

In 1942, MacDonald made her last two starring films for M-G-M: *I Married An Angel* with Nelson Eddy and *Cairo*, a war spy movie, co-starring Robert Young. Miss MacDonald's contract at M-G-M was not extended after 1942. Perhaps the studios began

This theater advertisement give-away was for the Jeanette MacDonald—Nelson Eddy M-G-M Technicolor film called *Bitter Sweet* from 1940.

The paper doll book called *Jeanette MacDonald Glorious Singing Star* published by Merrill Publishing Co. in 1941, #3460.

Screen Romances May, 1942 features a full page ad and the story and pictures from the M-G-M film, *I Married An Angel*, the final MacDonald—Eddy film.

This coloring book called, *Jeanette MacDonald Costume Parade* was published by Merrill Publishing Co. in 1941, #3461. The book also contains a paper doll and one outfit made from paper instead of cardboard.

taking more interest in younger stars like Lana Turner, Betty Grable, and Rita Hayworth, but Jeanette always thought her contract was not renewed because she had a quarrel with Mayer that was never resolved.

The era of Nelson Eddy and Jeanette MacDonald ended with the *I Married An Angel* film in 1942 but collectors covet any item that pictures the two stars together. Movie posters or lobby cards from these famous movies are very collectible but they are also very expensive. Ordinary fans, however, can still afford MacDonald-Eddy movie sheet music, movie fan magazines, and autographs of the two stars. Even though it was rumored that MacDonald and Eddy didn't even like each other, and most critics called Nelson Eddy a "wooden" actor, they must have been doing something right. Most of the team's eight movie musicals were successful at the box office and these films have certainly earned the two stars a deserved place in movie history.

In 1942, MacDonald left films for radio, concerts, and recordings. Like most Hollywood stars, Jeanette also did her part for the war effort. MacDonald did a United States tour during World War II for the Army Emergency Relief fund raising $94,681.87 for the cause. Her husband, Gene Raymond, was one of the first Hollywood actors to enlist in the armed forces. He became a captain in the United States Air Force and served his country well.

Movie Story for November, 1942 published the story of *Cairo* the M-G-M MacDonald movie.

This picture cut from a concert program has been autographed by Nelson Eddy, Jeanette MacDonald's frequent co-star.

March 3, 1931.

Dear Miss Manson:

I greatly appreciate your assistance in helping to arrange the program which I am broadcasting during the Camel Pleasure Hour, Wednesday evening, March 11th.

Needless to say, your letter pleases me very much.

I sincerely hope that you will enjoy the program, which, according to present plans, will include "Beyond the Blue Horizon".

Sincerely yours,

Jeanette MacDonald

I am going to sing over the radio in the near future.
You can help arrange my program by telling me what songs you would like to hear me sing.
Write to me at
THE NATIONAL BROADCASTING CO.
711 Fifth Avenue
New York, N. Y.

Thank you for your cooperation,
Jeanette MacDonald

This signed letter from Miss MacDonald was about plans for a radio program for 1931.

Jeanette McDonald poster used to promote a concert she was giving to help the Army Emergency Relief fund during World War II.

trying to escape from troubles caused by the worst economic depression in our history. For whatever reason, Jeanette MacDonald is still remembered by her fans with fondness and affection.

For Interested Fans:

Jeanette MacDonald International Fan Club
1617 SW Indian Trail
Topeka, KS 66604-1951

Four large publications each year
Club offers items for sale plus Yearly convention in Hollywood

A 78 RPM record album called *Jeanette MacDonald's Operetta Favorites* produced by RCA Victor in the mid-1940s.

In addition to her concerts, Miss MacDonald made her grand opera debut in *Romeo and Juliet* in Montreal and also appeared with the Chicago Civic Opera in *Faust* during her film hiatus. MacDonald's recording efforts began with RCA Victor in 1929 and she continued making records for them throughout her career. One 78 RPM record album, *Jeanette MacDonald's Operetta Favorites*, included songs from both *The Firefly* and the *Sweethearts* movies.

Jeanette MacDonald returned to films in 1944 for a guest spot in the Universal movie called, *Follow the Boys*. Then she worked for M-G-M where she played mature roles in several movies including *Three Daring Daughters* in 1947, *The Birds and the Bees* in 1948, and *The Sun Comes Up* in 1949. In *Three Daring Daughters*, Jeanette played the mother of M-G-M's new singing star Jane Powell.

Perhaps Jeanette realized a new cycle had begun because she bowed out of movies for good. She then performed infrequently as a television guest or in a night club act until health problems forced her to retire. Jeanette died of a heart attack in 1965 with her husband of nearly thirty years at her side.

Although Jeanette MacDonald never won an Oscar and certainly isn't considered one of America's finest actresses or singers, she did have qualities that made her as memorable as some Hollywood superstars. Perhaps it was the twinkle in her eye, her vivacious behavior, her lovely red-gold hair, or maybe just the hours of pleasure and pure entertainment she gave to Americans

Lobby card from the M-G-M movie, *Three Daring Daughters* from 1947 in which Jeanette MacDonald played the mother of new M-G-M singing star Jane Powell.

Charlie McCarthy
(And Edgar Bergen)

This composition Charlie McCarthy doll was made by the Effanbee Doll Co. beginning in 1937. The doll is 15″ tall and is all original. He has painted hair and eyes. The doll is marked on the back: "Edgar Bergen's Charlie McCarthy, An EFFanBEE product."

The name, Charlie McCarthy, immediately conjures up the picture of a top hatted wooden figure dressed in a fancy tux with a monocle in his eye. What a strange looking character to have instantly captured the affections of both children and adults. Even stranger is the fact that Charlie, as Edgar Bergen's ventriloquist dummy, was one of the biggest radio stars of all time,—a medium that consisted only of sound. The radio listeners had seen pictures of Charlie so they knew what he looked like and it was easy for them to imagine that the words Bergen said in Charlie's voice were really spoken by the wooden character. Perhaps it was even easier to believe Charlie was a real boy when the radio audience couldn't see Bergen's lips moving. The team's radio programs were far more successful than their movies so the reality of seeing Bergen work closely with Charlie in the films may have destroyed some of the illusion.

Edgar Bergen and Charlie McCarthy had a very unique career that went from vaudeville, to radio, to movies, to television, to night clubs over a period of fifty-six years. It began when Edgar Bergen was still in high school. He had become interested in ventriloquism and decided to develop an act, using a wooden dummy. He made a sketch of the kind of head he wanted to have made which he modeled after a local newspaper boy. A man named Mack carved the head for him and Bergen named his new partner Charlie after the newsboy and McCarthy for the woodcarver. He used his new dummy in an act he developed for local activities in Decatur, Illinois and Chicago.

Bergen began college at Northwestern University but the possibility of a vaudeville career caused him to drop his studies to become a full-time performer. Bergen did eventually receive a degree from Northwestern University in 1937. It was an honorary degree called the "Master of Innuendo and Snappy Comeback."

Edgar Bergen and Charlie McCarthy spent ten years as a vaudeville team. They traveled all over the world and eventually played the Palace in New York in 1930.

In 1936, Bergen took his friend Charlie for a guest appearance on the very popular Rudy Vallee radio show. Their act was such a hit, they guested for three more months. To publicize the two radio stars, valentines were produced which showed Charlie McCarthy on one card and Rudy Vallee on the other. These must have been printed in 1936 during the time Bergen and McCarthy were guests on the Vallee program.

In 1937 Bergen started his own show sponsored by Chase and Sanborn. The program was so successful that it was the number one rated show in the United States for two and a half years. Even as late as 1945 the program was in fifth place after having been on the air for eight years. The supporting cast for the show was also excellent. Don Ameche was the master of ceremonies, the singer

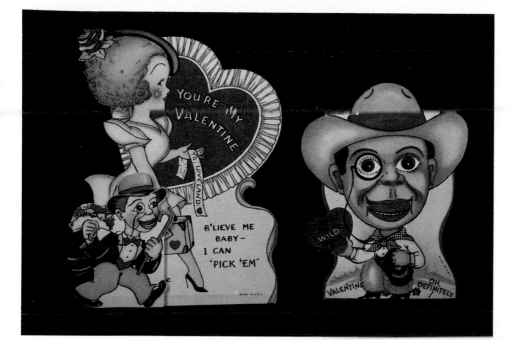

Charlie McCarthy was a popular Valentine character for companies in the later 1930s. These two cards date from that time period.

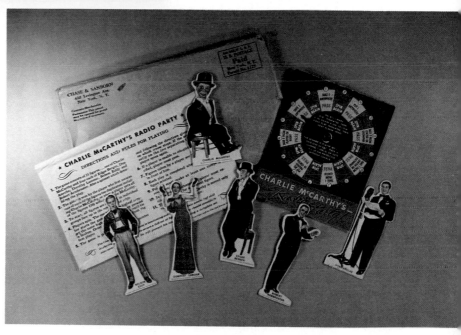

This radio premium game called *Charlie McCarthy's Radio Party* is from 1938. It includes the original Chase and Sanborn mailing envelope. The game features program regulars Edgar Bergen, Charlie McCarthy, Nelson Eddy, Don Ameche, Robert Armbruster, and Dorothy Lamour.

was Nelson Eddy and Ray Noble led the orchestra. A radio premium game was offered to the listeners by the Chase and Sanborn Co. It featured images of many of the program regulars and now is quite collectible.

The comedian W. C. Fields was a frequent guest on the show from 1937-1939. The "on the air" feud between Charlie and Fields provided material for many of the best programs from the series for those years. The radio success was transferred to the movie screen when Edgar Bergen and Charlie made their movie debut in *The Goldwyn Follies* in 1938.

In 1939, W. C. Fields, Edgar Bergen and Charlie McCarthy all starred in the movie, *You Can't Cheat An Honest Man* to take advantage of their radio show feud publicity. Charlie and Fields also traded barbs in this funny movie. The film is now available on video cassette so current fans can make the acquaintance of the unusual wooden boy.

Because of the great popularity of his radio show, all kinds of products were developed to tie in with Charlie's well-known image. Charlie was 38″ tall, weighed 40 pounds and was always supposed to be fourteen years old.

Many McCarthy toys were made during the late 1930s. One of the most expensive for collectors is the Charlie McCarthy doll produced by the Effanbee Doll Co. It was made in 1937 and has a composition head, hands, and feet, and a cloth body. The hair is molded and the eyes are painted. Many "look alike" Charlie dolls were also produced during this same period. These unofficial dolls are sometimes referred to as Charlie McCarthy dolls by unknowledgeable dealers. However these copies, even in excellent condition and in original clothing are not as highly valued since they do not carry the necessary Edgar Bergen endorsement. These tie-ins brought in a lot of money during the height of Charlie's popularity. Tie-in revenues were estimated to total $75,000 a year during a time when this country was still experiencing the terrible depression of the 1930s.

The sheet music from Edgar Bergen and Charlie McCarthy's first movie called *The Goldwyn Follies* made by Samuel Goldwyn in 1938. The song is called "Love Walked In" by George and Ira Gershwin. It was published by Chappell and Co. and was copyrighted by Gershwin Publishing Co.

This is an unlicensed look-alike Charlie McCarthy doll. The doll has a composition head and hands and a cloth body just like the real Charlie doll but this doll is unmarked. It is 20″ tall. Both dolls have mouths that can be moved using a string in the back.

This ad for the RKO movie called *You Can't Cheat An Honest Man* appeared in the *Screen Guide* magazine for February, 1939. The movie starred Charlie, Edgar and W. C. Fields and was made in 1939.

A later version of the ventriloquist's Charlie McCarthy doll was made by the Juro Co. for several years in the 1970s. It is 30″ tall and has a vinyl head and hands, cloth body, and molded hair. It is dressed in a tuxedo and has a string in the back to work the mouth. It sold for from $9.97 to $14.97 during the years it was produced.

Other expensive items for collectors are the Charlie McCarthy metal walker wind-up toy and the Charlie wind-up car. Other hard to find Charlie tie-ins include radios and watches made during the later 1930s in Charlie's image.

There are, however, lots of Charlie collectibles that are more affordable to the average collector. Perhaps books are the most easily found at reasonable prices. Picture books like *A Day With Charlie McCarthy*, published by Whitman Publishing Co. in 1938 are very reasonably priced. Big Little Books and coloring books, which are about McCarthy, may run a little higher but are still affordable. Charlie was also featured in a comic book published by Dell Publishing in the late 1940s. These comics offer an interesting collectible for a moderate investment for today's collector.

Paper doll books will be more expensive, especially if they are uncut. The paper dolls were published by Whitman Publishing Co. in 1938, and are titled *Edgar Bergen's Charlie McCarthy and His Hollywood Wardrobe*.

A puzzle was also made at the height of the little fellow's popularity. It was also produced by Whitman in 1938 and is called, *Edgar Bergen's Charlie McCarthy Picture Puzzles*. The Whitman Co. also manufactured a Charlie McCarthy game that same year called *Edgar Bergen's Charlie McCarthy Game of*

**This Charlie McCarthy Radio
Is Just One of Fifty Prizes!**

Look at these prizes: Each person writing
one of the ten best letters will receive a
table-model Charlie McCarthy radio as illustrated above; eleventh prize is $15.00 cash;
twelfth is $10.00 cash; thirteenth, $5.00 cash,
and the fourteenth to fiftieth prizes will be
other swell Charlie McCarthy novelties!

Screen Guide for February, 1939 pictures a Charlie McCarthy radio to be given away as one of the prizes in a contest.

A later version of the Charlie McCarthy doll made by the Juro Co. in the 1970s. It is made of vinyl and cloth. The mouth can also be moved on this doll by pulling a string located in the back of the doll.

This 8″ tall Charlie McCarthy tin wind up toy is called "The McCarthy Strut." It was made by Louis Marx and Co. in the late 1930s. The figure moves along as his mouth opens and closes. He is shown with the original box.

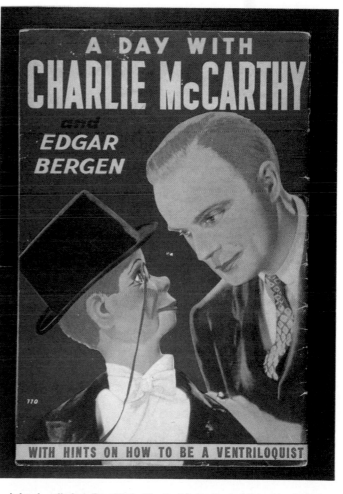

A book called *A Day With Charlie McCarthy* published by Whitman Publishing Co. in 1938.

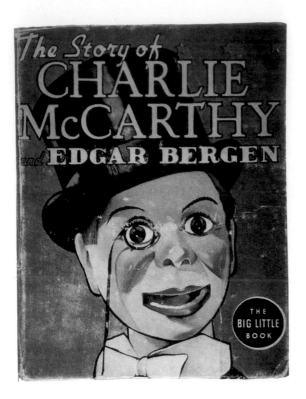

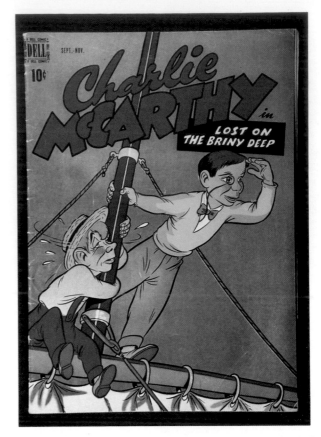

This Big Little Book titled *The Story of Charlie McCarthy* was published by Whitman Publishing Co. in 1938.

Dell Publishing Co. was responsible for a series of Charlie McCarthy comic books beginning in 1949. This is the September—November issue from 1949. The title is *Charlie McCarthy in Lost On the Briny Deep.*

These paper dolls of Charlie McCarthy were published in 1938 by the Whitman Publishing Co. They were called *Edgar Bergen's Charlie McCarthy and His Hollywood Wardrobe.* The set had four dolls and clothing.

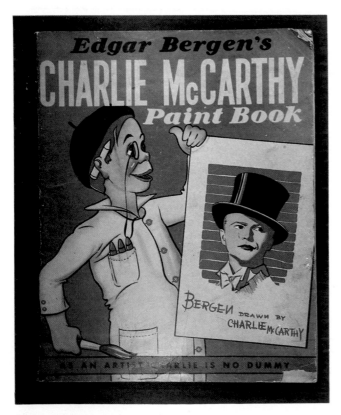

Whitman also published a paint book called *Edgar Bergen's Charlie McCarthy Paint Book* in 1938.

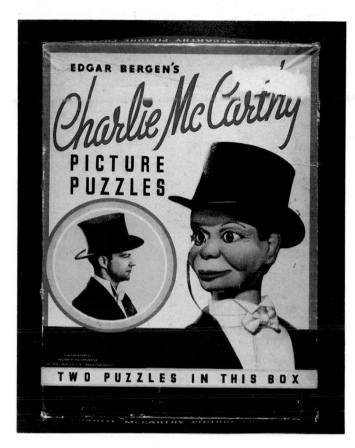

Edgar Bergen's Charlie McCarthy Question and Answer Game was also produced by Whitman in 1938. It is a card game with no game board.

This picture puzzle of Charlie McCarthy was made by Whitman in 1938. The box contained two puzzles.

Edgar Bergen's Charlie McCarthy Game of Topper was produced by the Whitman Publishing Co. in 1938. The game consists of a cardboard game board, a deck of cards featuring Charlie's likeness, and eight wooden top hats.

Topper. Other games made in Charlie's image include: *Edgar Bergen and Charlie McCarthy Flying Hats* produced by Whitman in 1938; *Charlie McCarthy Questions and Answers* game and *Charlie McCarthy Put and Take Bingo Game* also published by Whitman.

Other less expensive Charlie items include handkerchiefs, scrapbooks, drinking glasses, Charlie talking greeting cards, and school composition books. Items costing more money would include Charlie pencil sharpeners, rings and pins.

Edgar and Charlie continued to make movies along with appearing on the radio show. Charlie was the star of *Charlie McCarthy Detective* in 1939 and a spoon was produced showing him in his detective hat. Another spoon was made as an advertising premium for Chase and Sanborn which pictured Charlie in his typical top hat. Another unusual premium offered during the height of Charlie's radio fame was a large cardboard figure of the ventriloquist dummy designed so the mouth could be made to move as if the figure is talking. A radio listener could order this premium for four Chase and Sanborn coffee labels. A smaller cardboard figure was distributed by Walt Disney Enterprises at about this same time and although the item looks like McCarthy, there is no identification to make it an authorized Charlie McCarthy collectible. All of the premiums were advertised on the radio show which was broadcast Sunday evenings on the NBC Red Network.

In 1941, the comedy team made another film called *Look Who's Laughing* for RKO. The movie starred Edgar Bergen, Charlie McCarthy and Lucille Ball.

The movie fan magazines, as well as the radio magazines, covered Charlie McCarthy just as though he was a real person. He is frequently pictured with beautiful girls since he was portrayed as a "skirt chaser" in the movies and on radio. Charlie was also the cover subject of many magazines including *Time*, *Movie Life*, *Literary Digest*, *Radio Guide*, and *Radio Mirror*.

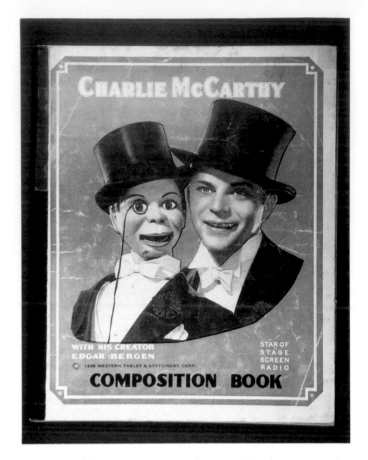

Even composition books were manufactured which featured Charlie's picture. This one was produced by the Western Tablet and Stationery Corp. in 1938.

This Charlie McCarthy spoon was made, as a Chase and Sanborn premium, to promote the new movie *Charlie McCarthy, Detective*. The spoon featured Charlie dressed in his detective hat and costume from the 1939 Universal film. Shown with the spoon is a picture of Charlie dressed for his movie role featured in *Song Hits* magazine for April 1940.

A Happy Birthday talking Charlie McCarthy card. When the piece of metal is run across a fingernail, it says "Happy Birthday". The card dates from 1938 and was patented by White and Wyckoff Mfg. Co.

148

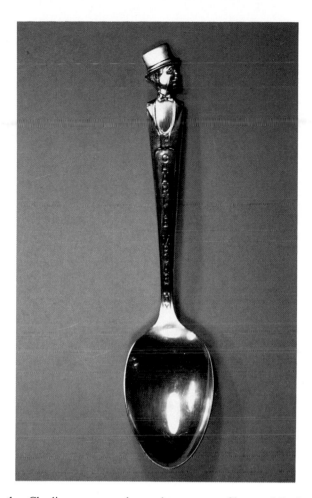

Another Charlie spoon was also used to promote Chase and Sanborn Coffee. For this spoon's design, Charlie is pictured in his more usual top hat.

A radio listener could order this Chase and Sanborn advertising premium with four coffee labels in the 1930s. The 21″ tall heavy cardboard figure is marked on the back "Patent Applied For Ketterlinus Phila and N. Y.". Charlie's mouth and eyes can be moved by a tab in his back and he is made so that he can sit.

A smaller 15″ tall McCarthy-like cardboard figure is stamped on the back, "Walt E. Disney Enterprises, LTD." Although the item is not identified as Charlie, the likeness is unmistakable. The arms and legs are made of corrugated paper so the limbs can be stretched as the paper is pulled.

149

Edgar Bergen was still doing his weekly radio show when *Radio Mirror* featured him with Charlie and his other partner Mortimer Snerd on the cover of their December, 1948 issue.

This movie poster was used to promote the movie, *Look Who's Laughing* which was produced in 1941 for RKO. Lucille Ball joined the fun in the film with Charlie and Edgar.

In 1942 Charlie and Edgar teamed up with other radio stars, Fibber McGee and Molly, to make the movie *Here We Go Again*. Then after a guest appearance in *Stage Door Canteen* in 1943, Edgar and Charlie made their last movie together in 1944. It was called, *Song of the Open Road* and co-starred Jane Powell. Although the team did not appear in any other films, Bergen played dramatic roles in several movies without his partner. These included *I Remember Mama* in 1948. Even though the Bergen-McCarthy movie career was over, the pair continued on radio until 1956. In 1947 Top Ten Records produced an interesting record album featuring several Bergen-McCarthy routines that had been part of their radio performances over a period of several years.

After their radio career ended, Edgar Bergen and Charlie McCarthy turned to television. Besides making guest appearances, they hosted the show "Do You Trust Your Wife?" on CBS from January, 1956 until March, 1957. After the program's demise, Bergen and Charlie limited their television participation to guest appearances. The team of Edgar Bergen and Charlie McCarthy received many honors during their heyday. In 1938, Charlie's hand and foot prints were placed in the cement of Grauman's Chinese Theater in Hollywood. The same year, Bergen received a special movie Oscar made of wood with a moving mouth for his special comedy contribution. Bergen also wrote the article on ventriloquism for the *Encyclopedia Britannica* since he was certainly considered an authority in the field.

This advertisement for the Charlie and Edgar movie from RKO Pictures *Here We Go Again* appeared in the *Movie Story* magazine for November, 1942. Other radio stars, Fibber McGee and Molly, were co-stars.

An Edgar Bergen-Charlie McCarthy record album was produced by the Top Ten Records in 1947. The four record album was done on 78 rpm records and featured several of the team's routines from earlier radio programs.

Edgar Bergen developed two other dummies for his act: Mortimer Snerd, the country bumpkin, and Effie Klinker, the old maid. Neither of them was as popular as Charlie McCarthy.

Edgar Bergen married rather late in life. He was thirty-nine years old when he met nineteen year old Frances Westerman and a year later (1945) they were married. They had two children, Candice born in 1946 and a son Kris born in 1961. Although Charlie McCarthy was always a part of the household, even having his own room, he was more involved in Candice's life than with her brother's. She has written an excellent book about this life called, *Knock Wood*. Candice participated in several of the radio shows as a youngster where she played herself.

Bergen worked with Charlie for fifty-six years. In 1978, he announced his coming retirement and scheduled a farewell engagement with Charlie in Las Vegas. The team received a standing ovation after each performance and critics said they were as funny as ever, even though much of the material was decades old. Mr. Bergen was seventy-five years old and after one of the shows, he went to sleep and just never woke up. What a fitting end for such a classy act!

Variety ran a cartoon the next morning with a drawing of Charlie showing a tear running down his cheek. Charlie McCarthy now has a home at the Smithsonian where he can still be seen by his fans. The old sparkle is missing, however, and we know he will never again say, "I'll mow you down, Bergen, so help me, I'll mow you down."

The last movie made by Edgar and Charlie was *Song of the Open Road* in 1944. The film was produced by Charles R. Rogers. The ad appeared in the *Modern Screen* magazine for July, 1944.

One of Margaret's M-G-M movies for 1948 was called *Tenth Avenue Angel* and it was featured in the *Screen Romance* magazine for November, 1946.

Margaret O'Brien's Book of Games and Fun was published in 1948 by the Barmaray Co. It is filled with pictures of Margaret as well as game and hobby ideas.

A 78 RPM record album from the film *The Unfinished Dance* was produced by M-G-M Records in 1947. Margaret's picture is featured on the cover.

This movie poster insert is from *The Secret Garden* which Margaret made in 1949 for M-G-M.

Margaret O'Brien's last big hit movie was made for M-G-M in 1949. It was *Little Women* co-starring June Allyson, Peter Lawford, Elizabeth Taylor and Janet Leigh along with Margaret. This window card pictures the all-star cast in the Louisa May Alcott favorite.

A lobby card from the O'Brien movie called *Her First Romance* from 1951. The movie was made for Columbia after Margaret's career had already peaked.

A window card for the O'Brien film called *Glory* from 1955. The horse picture was produced by RKO Pictures, Inc. Walter Brennan and Charlotte Greenwood were also in the movie

Miss O'Brien has kept busy with her acting, through the years, appearing mainly on television and in stock productions. She has been married and divorced and is a mother. Unlike many young stars, Margaret's money was invested and put in a trust so she received $250,000 when she came of age.

Margaret O'Brien, as an adult is quite generous in autographing portraits of herself, and fans may want to contact her in order to add a picture to their collections.

Although her successful career as a popular child star only lasted five or six years, Margaret will always be remembered by collectors and movie buffs as the child she once was. It is easy to picture her as the little girl riding with the ice man in *Meet Me in St. Louis* seriously discussing plans for her doll's funeral. To fans, Margaret will remain the child whose photograph appears on the postcard sent from the M-G-M studios to this author during the war year of 1944.

This postcard photo of the child star, Margaret O'Brien, was sent to fans (including this author) during the war year of 1944.

This photograph was autographed by Margaret after she was an adult.

160

Will Rogers
Ambassador of Goodwill

This picture of Will Rogers was used by the Frisco Railroad to promote their train named after the star. This souvenir was given to passengers who were traveling from St. Louis to San Francisco.

Will Rogers was one of America's greatest humorists as well as its ambassador of goodwill. Whenever there was a flood, earthquake or other disaster, he would be on his way to help out with both entertainment and financial assistance. He flew more than 500,000 miles in the last seven years of his life.

Rogers and his friend, flier Wiley Post, were on a flying trip in Alaska when their plane crashed and both men were killed near Point Barrow, Alaska in August of 1935. The two popular Oklahomans were eulogized by fellow countrymen from all walks of life, from the President to former Oklahoma neighbors.

Will Rogers always considered himself "just folks" and that is the way his fans thought of him as well. His humor touched everyone through radio, the movies, and his newspaper columns.

He could get by with kidding both Congress and the President, and the American people loved him for it.

Rogers was born in Oklahoma in what is now the small town of Oolagah, but was still Indian Territory in 1879 when he arrived. The nearest town of any size was Claremore about twelve miles away. Will was always proud of the fact that he was one quarter Cherokee Indian. The area around Claremore was cattle country and Will grew up on a ranch. He loved being around horses, and learned to rope as well as ride.

Schooling was never one of Rogers' top priorities. Although he attended several schools, he gave up formal education entirely when he sneaked out of the Kemper Military Academy at Boonville, Missouri during his junior year and headed for Texas cow country. After stints as a cow puncher and cattle driver, Will returned home to Oklahoma to help run the family ranch. When he had sold some cattle and made $2,000 profit, he talked a friend into heading out to South America with him to begin to see the world. After finally reaching their destination (via England) his companion left him to return home and Will went back to working with cows for a living. When he tired of South America, Will worked his way across the ocean on a steamer to South Africa where he secured a part, doing rope tricks, in Texas Jack's Wild West Show. After also sampling show business in Australia in the Wirth Brothers Circus, he returned to the United States and Oklahoma by way of San Francisco. Being broke, as usual, Will had to hop a freight train to make it home. He was twenty-three years old when he returned and his father was afraid he would never settle down.

In 1904 when a new siege of restlessness overtook Will, he went to the St. Louis World's Fair where he participated in another wild west show. When, sometime later, the leader of the enterprise, Zach Mulhall, wanted to try the same kind of show in New York, Will Rogers was raring to go.

The show folded after a short stand in Madison Square Garden and Rogers decided to stay in New York and try show business on his own. With his horse and his lariat as props, Will and a friend put together an act, which was booked into Hammerstein's Theater for a try-out. It was a moderate success and Rogers continued to play vaudeville houses. At first he let the rope tricks speak for themselves and didn't say anything at all in the act. One night when the audience wasn't being duly impressed with one of the difficult tricks, Rogers decided to explain to them what he was trying to do. With his humor showing through his basic explanation, the audience loved his talk and they laughed in appreciation. The humorist in Will began to take over the act. Although he kept on doing rope tricks, he devoted more and more time in his presentation to his monologue. When he ran out of jokes, he started reading the daily newspapers and commented humorously on what was happening in the news. He often started his act by saying, "All I know is what I read in the papers everyday." After much practice and years spent in many different engagements, his act eventually became a hit and he moved up to become one of the stars of the Ziegfeld Follies in 1914. It was his comedy as much as his rope tricks that had made him successful.

Will Rogers married Betty Blake in 1908 when he was twenty-nine years old. Betty had been a friend from his days in Oklahoma, although her own home was in Arkansas. Their courtship had been rather sporadic through the years and during some of the time Will had been away from home, they hadn't even kept in touch.

With the success Rogers had in the Follies, he was persuaded to try his luck in Hollywood by making a silent movie for Samuel Goldwyn in 1918. The movie was called *Laughing Bill Hyde*. It was followed by twelve other silent films including *A Texas Steer* all made during the next ten years. None of the films was particularly successful and most of them were not preserved so they cannot be seen today. Roger's personality and humor depended on sound and without his voice, he just didn't come across as the great comedian he was.

Rogers accepted his failure and returned to New York to work in the Follies. In 1922 he was approached by the McNaught Newspaper syndicate to write a humorous column to be sent to papers all over the country. Although Will was interested, it took him a while to hit on an idea that would work for him. He eventually did the column pretty much as he did his act, by using topical humor that he took from newspaper stories. Before his death, 500 newspapers printed the approximately 100 words he wrote every day and his longer weekly Sunday columns did just as well. He eventually made about $2500 each week just from his newspaper work. Rogers typed his column each day on a portable typewriter he kept in his car. He usually sat in the front seat of the car while he worked, with his feet on the running board. He used only two fingers to type and did his copy in all capital letters with little punctuation. He always worked in the morning and usually sent out his columns by telegraph. Many newspaper columnists would consider this a full time job but Rogers did his writing along with making movies, doing lectures, performing in benefits, and participating in any other engagements in which he had become involved.

With this success, Rogers became known as "America's Greatest Humorist" and he continued making personal appearances as he had done in vaudeville. One of these "one night stands" occurred in Coffeyville, Kansas just a few miles from his home in Oolagah.

In 1928 Will Rogers did a good turn for a friend that has been remembered all these years. Fred Stone, a Broadway star of musical comedy, was injured in a plane accident just a short while before his new play called *Three Cheers* was to open on Broadway. Rogers called Stone offering to take his place in the show until the injured man could take over. The producer, Charles Dillingham, accepted the offer. Since Rogers was not a musical star, he changed the show to fit his character-leaving in the musical numbers and doing his own kind of humor as his contribution to the production. The show was saved and Dillingham always sent him a blank check for his pay so Rogers could fill in whatever salary he felt he deserved.

In 1929, Will Rogers was forty-nine years old. He and his wife Betty had three children, Will Jr., Mary and Jimmy. Rogers was making a good living on the stage and with his newspaper writing but he was not yet the "American Goodwill Ambassador" he would become.

Pictured is a postcard scene from a Will Rogers silent film called *A Texas Steer*, a First National picture from 1928.

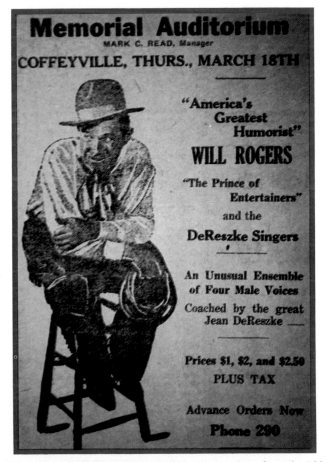

This ad for a Will Rogers's personal appearance dates from the 1930s. Rogers was known as "America's greatest humorist" and he was able to draw crowds even in small towns at prices from $1.00 to $2.50 which was a lot of money in those times.

Talking motion pictures changed all that. The Fox Film Corporation made him a good offer to return to Hollywood for another try at films. With the new sound equipment making it possible for the American public to hear Rogers' own peculiar brand of speech as well as to see him, the film producers thought they might be able to make a movie hit with Rogers as the star.

A novel by Homer Croy, an author from a small midwestern town, was selected as Rogers' first film story. Croy, himself, wrote the script (with help from Will). The vehicle was called *They Had To See Paris* and when the film was finished, Will Rogers had, at last, made a hit movie.

With the success of his first talkie, Rogers started making movies as fast as possible. The producers had found the right combination for Will's movie career, and by 1933 he had already made nine talkies. That was the year he made one of his best, *State Fair*. The movie starred Janct Gaynor along with Will. A jigsaw puzzle was produced showing a scene from the film. This type of item offers a fine addition to a movie collection of early film lore.

Other successful Rogers' films for Fox included: *Mr. Skitch*; *Connecticut Yankee*; *Ambassador Bill*; *Steamboat Round the Bend*; *In Old Kentucky*; and *Doubting Thomas*.

The Rogers-Fox film *Lightnin'* was promoted in this ad which appeared in *New Movie* magazine in February, 1931.

Shown is an advertisement which appeared in *Screen Book* magazine. It is for Will Rogers's first talking picture, *They Had To See Paris*. The film was made by Fox Film Corporation in 1929.

This jigsaw puzzle is of a Rogers scene from the hit Fox film called *State Fair* which was made in 1933. The puzzle cost twenty-five cents when it was new.

A still from the Will Rogers Fox Film called *Doubting Thomas* which was made during the last year of his life. Billie Burke, Allison Skipworth, Sterling Holloway, Gail Patrick and Frances Grant were in the movie.

Lobby card from the Rogers film called *Mr. Skitch* from 1933 which was made by Fox. Seated with Will in the car is Zasu Pitts.

With Will's success as a movie star now assured, it was time for him to try a new medium—radio. As the depression dragged on, the American people were devoting more and more time to free entertainment and that included radio. Rogers began making regular appearances on the new medium and these programs, too, brought more fame to the folksy philosopher. A magazine called *Radio Stars* from 1933 featured Will Rogers as the cover subject. Rogers' radio performances can still be heard by today's fans with cassettes produced by Radio Reviews. Rogers continued to be a participant in radio broadcasts throughout his life and he earned around $60,000 from the medium in the year before he died.

Along with his radio broadcasts, Rogers continued his movie making. The movie, *David Harum*, in 1934, provided Rogers with his first screen kiss. He was not fond of love scenes in his movies so no one told him about the kiss. When his co-star Louise Dresser suddenly kissed him, he blushed with surprise to give a true-to-character screen performance.

Will Rogers had a reputation for providing his own dialogue in his movies. He would have the director give him the sense of what the scene was all about and then he would use his own words to carry the story forward. In fact, Will Rogers was able to connect with movie-going audiences because, basically, he played himself in every picture. Many of the Rogers' movies are now available on video cassette including *Judge Priest* from 1934.

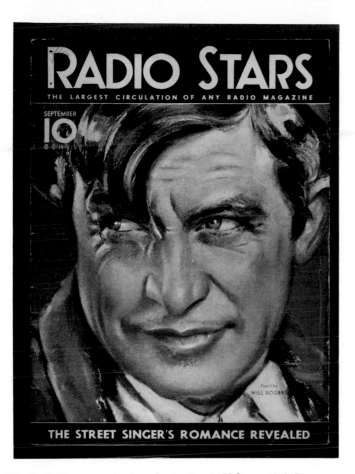

The *Radio Stars* magazine from September, 1933 features Will Rogers on its cover.

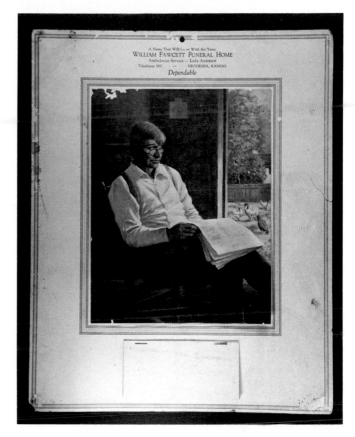

Will Rogers calendars were popular customer give-aways both during Will's life and after his death. The William Fawcett Funeral Home in Neodesha, Kansas distributed this calendar for 1942.

Will played the part of the Ambassador of Good Will for many businesses by letting them use his face to promote their firms. This fan was given away by the Boyd Roland Funeral Home in Corning, Iowa.

From 1931 until 1935, Rogers was among the top ten box office stars in Hollywood. In 1933, 1934, and 1935 he was the top male star and in 1934 he was the top star of male or female. His folksy humor and unusual personality carried all the twenty-two sound movies he made.

Because of this success, businesses began to pay to use his likeness to promote their firms. Collectors can look for items like fans and calendars to add interest to a Will Rogers collection. Many other products were also sold which featured the Rogers' image to tie-in to his popularity.

Will Rogers was a very versatile person. He liked to play polo when he wasn't working and he had several ponies on his ranch near Santa Monica. He also loved to travel and always flew whenever possible. During his trips, he was a guest in the White House many times, accepting invitations from three different presidents, Coolidge, Hoover, and Roosevelt. Even though Rogers earned over $1500 a day from 1931 until 1935, he always remained "The Cherokee Kid" and never forgot his roots, making frequent trips home to the ranch in Oklahoma.

After his tragic death in 1935, Will Rogers was buried in Forest Lawn Cemetery near Los Angeles after a private funeral. Four Cherokee Indians drove from Oklahoma and sat in the reserved space with Rogers' relatives. Many of the floral pieces were fashioned to resemble chaps, lariats, and saddles. Several other services for Rogers were held at the various movie studios. John Boles sang "Old Faithful" (a cowboy's song to his horse) during one memorial.

The Weather

The Tulsa Tribune
The Quality Newspaper of the West

FINAL
SPORT
EDITION

Will Rogers, Wiley Post Instantly
Killed as Plane Crashes in Alaska

Famous Flier, Beloved Humorist, Favorite Sons of Oklahoma, Killed

Craft Carrying Oklahoma
Famous Humorist, Noted
Flier Falls Near Pt. Barrow

Aerial Vacationists Were Flying From Fairbanks to Northernmost White Settlement in America When Globe Girdler's New Plane Plunges Only 50 Feet to Icy Ground; Motor Trouble, Fog Blamed for Accident; Bodies May Be Returned to Homes by Lindbergh

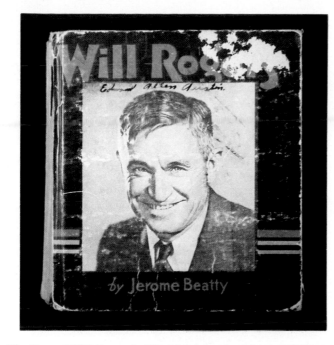

The Story of Will Rogers (a "Big Little" type book) was published by Saalfield Publishing Co. in 1935 as a tribute to Rogers after his death.

This 13" tall metal lamp base is marked on the base "No. 234". The base is in the shape of a globe with a molded airplane at its top. The faces of Will Rogers and Wiley Post are modeled in relief on the front of the lamp. The names of the two men are engraved on the base of the lamp. The lamp was evidently manufactured shortly after the plane crash which killed the two men in 1935. The lamp is finished in copper.

This postcard of the Rogers statue is from the 1930s. It is a Curteich—Chicago C.T. American Art Postcard. Across the top it says, "Oklahoma's Memorial to Will Rogers, Claremore, Okla."

Pictured is the folder given to passengers on the Frisco Railroad. Inside was a large picture of Will along with a copy of the official Will Rogers poem that was cast in bronze and is located at the Will Rogers Memorial in Claremore, Oklahoma.

Warner Brothers produced a movie about Will Rogers in 1952 in which
his son, Will Rogers Jr., played the title role. Pictured is a lobby card from
the film which was titled, *The Story of Will Rogers.*

This 12″ tall Will Rogers chalk statue was made after his death. At the
bottom of the figure is printed "I never met a man I didn't like 1879-Will
Rogers-1935."

Shirley Temple
Our Dimpled Darling

Pictured are some of the many Shirley Temple collectibles a fan can accumulate. The most expensive item shown is the large composition doll wearing her original clothing. She is 29" tall. Another 15" tall composition doll as well as a 12" tall vinyl Shirley doll from the late 1950s are also pictured. All the dolls were made by the Ideal Novelty and Toy Co. The books include: *Little Colonel* #1095 published by Saalfield in 1935 and *The Littlest Rebel* published by Random House in 1959. The sheet music of "On the Good Ship Lollipop" was published by Sam Fox Publishing Co.

In 1934, during the midst of the worst depression this world has ever known, America fell in love with a tiny golden haired moppet: Shirley Temple. Now, nearly sixty years later, some people are still actively pursuing their love affair with Shirley by collecting Shirley Temple memorabilia.

Shirley was born on April 23, 1928 in Santa Monica, California. Her parents, George and Gertrude, had already been blessed with two sons, so the addition of a darling little girl to the family was most welcome.

Mrs. Temple found that, even as a toddler, Shirley loved to dance to the music on the radio. As a result she enrolled her in dancing school at the Meglin Dance Studios in Los Angeles when she was only three. It was while Shirley was a pupil at the school that the movie scout Charles Lamont from Educational Studios chose her to appear in short films to be made by that studio. The shorts featured children spoofing first run movies. As Shirley

Temple began her film career she was paid $10 per day for four days of work on each short in the series called "Baby Burlesk."

Shirley's charm in these films caught the attention of Leo Houch, who was an assistant director for Fox Film Corp., and he gave her a starring role in *Stand Up and Cheer* in 1934. Shirley's golden curls and her pleasing personality made her an instant hit with the public so she was signed to a seven year contract with Fox for $150 per week.

The studio took advantage of their tiny star's success and she made twelve movies in the year of 1934 alone. They included: *Now I'll Tell* (Fox Film Corp.), *Little Miss Marker* (Paramount), *Change of Heart* (Fox Film Corp.), *Baby Take a Bow* (Fox Film Corp.), *Now and Forever* (Paramount), *Bright Eyes* Fox Film Corp.), and *The Little Colonel* (Fox Film Corp.). Although Shirley did not have leading parts in all these films, several of her most successful pictures were produced during the year. These included: *Baby Take a Bow* co-starring James Dunn; *The Little Colonel* with Shirley's first teaming with Bill Robinson and *Bright Eyes* co-starring Jane Withers. Jane Withers was a perfect contrast to light, sweet, dimpled Shirley as she was dark, rather plain and tom boyish. Shirley's famous song from this film "On the Good Ship Lollipop" sold over 400,000 copies of sheet music.

Because of all these movies and the great box office receipts they produced, Shirley's contract for Fox was renegotiated during 1934. Shirley was to be paid $1,250 per week with her mother to receive an additional $150 per week to be with Shirley on the set. Her picture production was cut as well and Shirley would only be expected to make three pictures per year instead of the twelve she had made in 1934.

There has never been such a popular child movie star as Shirley Temple. Her good looks and talent made her a perfect role model for little girls all over the world. Mother's began shaping their own little girls' hair into ringlets in an attempt to copy Shirley's look. The short dresses with full skirts and ruffles Shirley wore in her movies were also imitated and it wasn't long until manufacturers were producing Shirley Temple endorsed clothing.

In fact all kinds of companies were trying to find a place for their products on the Shirley Temple bandwagon. Because of all the Shirley endorsement activity, collectors of Shirley memorabilia have many items from which to choose when building a collection.

Some of the most desirable of the Shirley endorsed products are the Shirley Temple dolls which have been made in several different designs through the years. The first dolls were made of all-composition by the Ideal Novelty and Toy Co. The dolls were produced from 1934 through the late 1930s. They came in many sizes including 11″, 13″, 15″, 18″, 20″, 25″ and 27″. The dolls had sleep eyes, open mouths with teeth and beautiful mohair wigs which featured the famous Temple curls. Because the dolls were rather expensive, other doll companies also made imitation Shirley Temple dolls but the dolls made by Ideal were the only ones authorized by Shirley Temple. A large 20″ Shirley sold for $10.50 when new. That was a lot of money for a doll during the depression years so most children were not able to own such a prize. The smaller 13″ doll sold for much less and was priced at under $3.00 when ordered by mail from Sears. Even $3.00 was too expensive for many children when cheaply made dolls could be purchased for $1.00 or less in those depression days.

Although most Shirley Temple dolls offered for sale were little girl models, the Ideal Co. also made a Baby Shirley Temple. The doll had a composition head, arms, and legs, and a cloth body. It came with either a blonde mohair wig or molded hair, sleep eyes, and an open mouth. There were two sizes of the doll, 16″ and 25″. Since there are fewer of these dolls available today, they are more expensive for collectors to purchase. The most desirable dolls are the mint dolls with original clothing, pins, and boxes. Those dolls, of course, are hard to find and, therefore, bring a top price.

Shirley Temple is pictured in a costume she wore in *The Little Colonel*, made by the Fox Film Corp. in 1934. The item comes from a scrapbook compiled by a fan of the 1930s who noted the date and place she had seen each Shirley movie.

"On Account-a I Love You" was sung by Shirley in *Baby Take a Bow*, the Fox Film Corp. movie made with James Dunn in 1934. Bud Green and Sam Stept were the composers. It was published by the Sam Fox Publishing Co.

This picture of Shirley was used by the Klock Theater in Neodesha, Kansas to advertise the Fox Film Corp. film, *Bright Eyes* made in 1934 with Jane Withers.

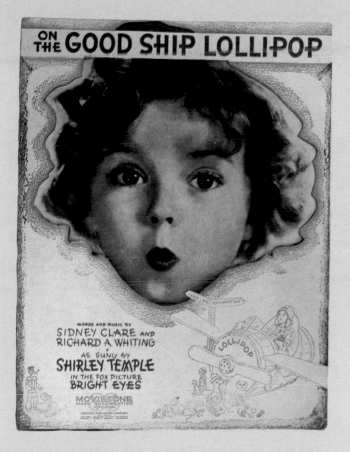

This is one of the most popular Temple songs, "On the Good Ship Lollipop" from Fox Film Corp.'s *Bright Eyes* in 1934. The song was by Sidney Clare and Richard Whiting. It was published by Sam Fox Publishing Co.

A labeled Shirley Temple child's dress made by Cinderella. It is yellow with brown dots. It belonged to a small girl in Iowa circa 1936. The dress was made by Rosenau Brothers, Inc.

This newspaper ad from Plattsburgh, New York shows several Shirley Temple dresses being advertised by Merkel's Department Store. The dresses are priced at $1.98 (circa 1936).

171

The same child also owned this Shirley Temple coat. The coat is red violet trimmed in brown fur. The label reads "Styled for Shirley Temple."

This is a 20″ tall all-composition Shirley Temple doll made by the Ideal Novelty and Toy Co. She has sleep eyes, a mohair wig, and an open mouth. She is wearing her all original green organdy dress with her original pin. the dress, head, and body are marked "Shirley Temple."

Sears winter catalog for 1935-1936 carried ads for both the Shirley Temple little girl dolls and the Shirley baby dolls. The girl dolls came in sizes 13″, 16″, 18″, and 20″. The baby dolls were 15½″, 18″ and 20″ sizes. The dolls were priced from $2.89 to $5.79. Dresses for the dolls could also be purchased for 94 cents to $1.59.

This is the original box for the 20″ tall Shirley Temple doll. It bears its original price tag of $10.50 which was quite a lot of money in those depression days.

172

This is the 13″ tall all-composition Shirley Temple doll by Ideal. The back of her head and her back are marked "Shirley Temple" and a "13" appears on her shoulders. She has sleep eyes, a mohair wig, and an open mouth with teeth. She wears her original clothing consisting of a pink pleated organdy dress, one piece underwear, shoes and socks.

The 16″ tall Shirley Temple baby doll was also made by the Ideal Novelty and Toy Co. beginning in 1935. She has a composition swivel head on a shoulder plate, composition arms and legs, and a cloth body with a crier in the back. Her hair is mohair and she has sleep eyes, an open mouth, and teeth. The back of her head is marked "Shirley Temple." Her clothing is original.

In addition to dolls, many other toys were manufactured to take advantage of Shirley's popularity. For collectors, the Shirley Temple paper dolls, produced in the 1930s, are high on the list of desirable Shirley collectibles. The first set of Shirley Temple paper dolls was published in 1934 by the Saalfield Co. which made all the Shirley paper dolls in the 1930s. It was called *Shirley Temple: Dolls and Dresses* #2112 and featured four dolls. As Shirley's success continued, other sets of paper dolls were made by Saalfield including: *Shirley Temple Playhouse*, #1739; *Shirley Temple Standing Dolls* (back and front), #1715, 1935; *Shirley Temple Standing Doll*, #1719, 1935; *Shirley Temple Standing Doll* (back and front), #1727, 1935; *Shirley Temple 34″ tall*, #1765, 1936; *Shirley Temple*, #1761, 1937; *Shirley Temple and Her Movie Wardrobe*, #1773, 1938; *Shirley Temple*, #1782, 1939; and *Shirley Temple Masquerade*, #1787, 1940. The uncut Shirley Temple paper dolls are the most desirable.

Besides paper dolls, other paper toys were made in Shirley's image by the Saalfield Co. during the 1930s. A collection of the various coloring books featuring Shirley would be far less expensive to pursue than a collection of paper doll books. Many different ones were produced and they are still priced reasonably. Unused mint books will be priced higher than used books. Some of the coloring books just featured a picture of Shirley on the front cover while the contents did not relate to Shirley. Many of the books did have pictures of Shirley throughout the book and those coloring books are the most desirable. Coloring books from the period include: *Shirley Temple Drawing Book*, 1935 #1725; *Shirley Temple Coloring Book*, 1935 #1735; and the *Shirley Temple Coloring Box* #1740.

By 1935, Shirley Temple was in the number one position among the top ten box office stars of the country. She would retain that spot through 1938. Her fan mail averaged 5,000 letters each

The first set of Shirley Temple paper dolls was made by the Saalfield
Publishing Co. in 1934. The book was called *Shirley Temple Dolls and
Dresses* #2112 and contained four dolls and clothing.

This is one of the most popular of the Shirley Temple paper doll sets
because the two dolls and clothing picture both the backs and fronts of
each item. Saalfield published the book in 1935 and it is #1715.

In 1936 Saalfield tried something different when they produced a large
life size Shirley Temple paper doll 34" tall. The book was called *Shirley
Temple: A Life-Like Paper Doll Cut-out;* #1765. The book also contained
a smaller doll.

174

The paper doll book called *Shirley Temple Dolls and Dresses* featured two large size Shirley paper dolls. It was published by Saalfield in 1937 and is #1761.

The last Shirley Temple paper doll book published during the 1930s was done by Saalfield in 1939. The book included two large dolls and clothing. It was #1782.

Another very popular Shirley paper doll set for today's collector is the book titled *Shirley Temple Dolls and Her Movie Wardrobe*. Many of her movie costumes are included in this fascinating paper doll book which is #1773 and was published in 1938. Two dolls are featured.

Saalfield produced many coloring books of Shirley over the years. This one is #1717 and dates from 1936. No pictures of Shirley are inside.

Another Shirley Temple coloring book was published by Saalfield in 1937. It is #1772 and also does not include Shirley pictures inside.

This is My Crayon Book: Shirley Temple is the title of another Saalfield coloring book published in 1935. The back of the book shows the back of the Shirley Temple figure. It is #1711 and the inside pages do not include pictures of Shirley.

week. The Academy of Arts and Sciences even presented her with a special Oscar for her film work in 1935. Fox also recognized their star's drawing ability by raising Shirley's salary once more to $5,000 each week.

Shirley Temple hit films for 1935 were *Our Little Girl*, *The Littlest Rebel*, and *Curly Top*. Because many of Shirley's films were musicals, sheet music from her movies adds interest to a Shirley Temple collection. These pieces usually feature Shirley's picture in a scene from the film. To take advantage of Shirley's musical talent, song books were also published which featured the words and music to these songs.

In 1936 the Temple popularity continued with more hit movies made for Twentieth Century-Fox. They included *Captain January*, in which Shirley co-starred with Guy Kibbee. Although Shirley usually carried each picture by herself, she did have a chance to work with Alice Faye in *Poor Little Rich Girl* and *Stowaway* in 1936. Shirley's other hit picture from 1936 was *Dimples* with Frank Morgan playing the part of her father.

Saalfield Publishing Co. began a practice of publishing a book featuring movie scenes for each of the hit Temple films. These paperback books have become collector's items because they not only tell the stories of her films but also supply pictures of Shirley and the other cast members.

This scene from *The Littlest Rebel* features Shirley Temple and one of her favorite dancing partners, Bill Robinson, from Shirley's Twentieth Century-Fox movie from 1935.

Our Little Girl, the Shirley—Fox film from 1935 was advertised in a New York newspaper for the RKO Palace Theater. Joel McCrea was Shirley's co-star.

Another of Shirley's very popular songs was "Animal Crackers in My Soup" featured in the *Curly Top* film from 1935. The writers were Ray Henderson, Ted Koehler, Edward Heyman, and Irving Caesar. It was published by Sam Fox Publishing Corp.

Movie herald for Shirley's *Captain January* film. It includes advertising from the Elroy Theater for May, 1936. The Twentieth Century-Fox movie teamed Shirley with Slim Summerville. Photograph courtesy of Daryl Christensen.

This song magazine called *Shirley Temple Song Album—No. 2* was published in 1936 by Sam Fox Publishing co.

Sing with Shirley Temple, a song album published by Movietone Music Corp. in 1935. The book featured many of Shirley's hit songs. Pictures of Shirley in her movie roles are also included.

The song "When I'm With You" by Mack Gordon and Harry Revel is from the Fox picture, *Poor Little Rich Girl*. The film, made in 1936, co-starred Alice Faye and Jack Haley. The music was published by the Robbins Music Corp. in 1936.

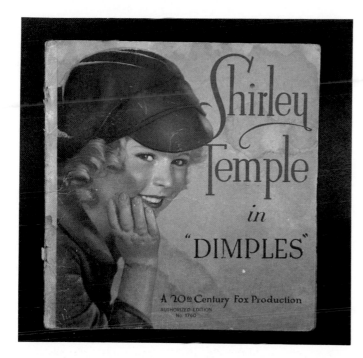

When Shirley was making the film *Dimples* for Fox in 1936, Saalfield published a tie-in book with the story and pictures from the movie.

Because of the interest in Shirley Temple, magazines began featuring stories about the young star. Today's collectors are usually interested in any of these articles but they are especially drawn to magazines that feature Shirley's picture on the cover. Many of the movie magazines of the period used Shirley Temple as their cover art including *Screenland* April, 1936; *Modern Screen* July, 1935, and May, 1936; *Photoplay* January, 1935; *New York Sunday News* June 12, 1938 and *Movie Mirror* December, 1934; February, 1938; May, 1940 and May, 1936. The inside photographs were often saved by early collectors and placed in scrapbooks that now also make very valuable additions to a Shirley Temple collection. Even the scrapbooks themselves could be purchased with pictures of Shirley Temple on the covers.

Besides books about Shirley's movies, Saalfield also published many books for children picturing Shirley in her every day life. They used several formats for these books including the well known "Big Little Book" look. Two of these books are called *The Story of Shirley Temple* and *My Life and Times*. Saalfield also used the style they had featured in their Shirley movie books with the books called *How I Raised Shirley Temple*, *Shirley Temple Through the Day*, and *The Real Little Girl and Her Honolulu Diary*. More unusual is the hardback book that was published by Saalfield in 1935 called *Shirley Temple*.

This sheet music comes from Shirley's Twentieth Century-Fox film *Stowaway* from 1936. The song is "Goodnight my Love" by Mack Gordon and Harry Revel. It was published by Robbins Music Corp.

Movie Mirror featured Shirley on their cover for February, 1938.

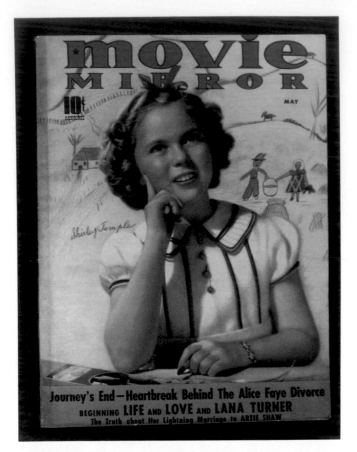

Movie Mirror for May, 1940 also used Shirley for its cover piece.

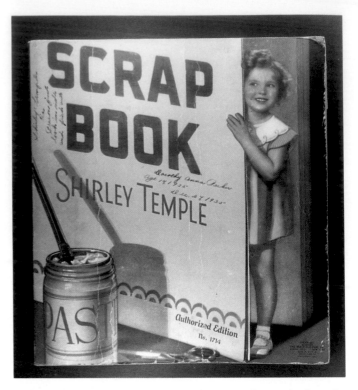

Saalfield published several different Shirley Temple scrapbooks so her fans could save clippings about the young star. This one is #1714 from 1935.

Photoplay magazine also used Shirley for the cover of their December, 1936 issue. The drawing was by James Montgomery Flagg.

In 1936 the same firm produced this scrapbook which an early fan used to hold Shirley pictures. It is #1722.

The Saalfield Publishing Co. published this "Big Little" style book in 1936. The title is *My Life and Times* by Shirley Temple as told to Max Trell. It is filled with photographs of Shirley Temple.

Shirley Temple Through the Day is another book by Saalfield filled with pictures of Shirley in her daily life. It was produced in 1936.

How I Raised Shirley Temple was published in 1935 by the Saalfield Publishing Co. It was based on an article from *Screenland* magazine and was filled with pictures of Shirley.

The Real Little Girl and her Honolulu Diary was the name of the book published by Saalfield about Shirley's daily life in 1938. It is divided into two parts—the first is about her regular life and the second part describes her family vacation trip to Honolulu.

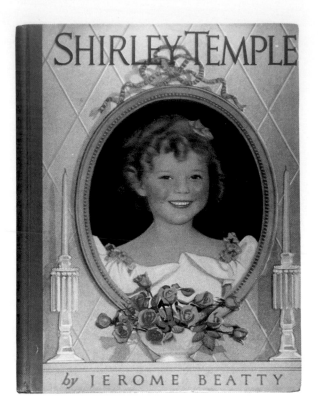

The Saalfield Co. also published a hardback book about Shirley Temple. It, too, is filled with pictures of Shirley. Jerome Beatty authored the book in 1935.

Because the Saalfield Publishing Co. discovered that any book sold better if it had a Shirley Temple connection, they began publishing books that really had nothing to do with Shirley except that these books featured Shirley's picture on the cover and sometimes the book also included photographs of Shirley throughout the publication. Examples of this practice are the books called *Shirley Temple's Favorite Poems* and *Shirley Temple Pastime Book*. An even stranger example of taking advantage of the Shirley name is the book called *Shirley Temple's Book of Fairy Tales*. The Saalfield Co. used a book exactly as it had been produced in 1922 and added a photograph of Shirley to the front cover and Shirley pictures throughout the book to make another marketable Shirley Temple book. The fairy tale illustrations were very old-fashioned by 1936 when the Shirley material was added. Another nicer Shirley promotion was a boxed set of five paperback books, all about Shirley Temple, packaged by Saalfield in 1936.

Many other tie-in items were manufactured in the 1930s to take advantage of Shirley's popularity. These products included anklets, hats, playing cards, soap, purses, pocket mirrors, pencil boxes, handkerchiefs, stationery, hair bows, pen and pencil sets, jewelry, tablets, doll dishes, doll trunks and doll buggies. The doll trunks and doll buggies are especially sought after by collectors.

Although Shirley Temple did not become involved in endorsing as many products as did the Dionne Quintuplets, her picture was used by both Quaker Puffed Wheat and Wheaties to advertise their products. Wheaties featured twelve different photographs of the young star on packages of the breakfast cereal. Shirley Temple premiums that could be obtained with the purchase of Wheaties

cereal included a blue cereal bowl, pitcher, and mug all featuring pictures of Shirley on the glass dishes. The pitcher is now being reproduced.

In 1937 Shirley's hits continued with *Wee Willie Winkie* and *Heidi*. As each new film was made, new products were distributed to take advantage of the movie's publicity. The Shirley dolls were dressed in costumes from the film and new books were marketed which told the story of each new movie.

By 1938 even magazines like *Life* were devoting space to the top star in the country. The July 11, 1938 issue featured Shirley as she toured across the country for a "vacation." The publicity surrounding this trip that Shirley made with her family was unending. Many scrapbooks from the period have preserved articles written about Shirley's adventures on her cross country excursion. A coloring book was also produced to present a record of this trip.

Shirley's fame made her home a "must see" attraction for tourists taking the bus tours of the Hollywood area. Postcards featuring her residence were sold to fans as a souvenir of their trip.

Shirley's films for the year 1938 continued to do well and she remained in her number one box office position. Her movies included: *Rebecca of Sunnybrook Farm*, *Just Around the Corner*, and *Little Miss Broadway*.

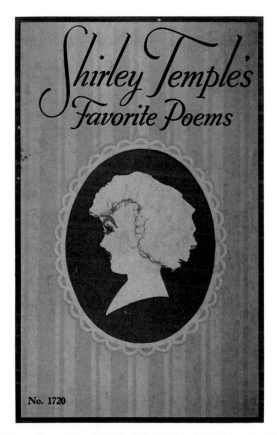

Saalfield brought out this unusual poetry book in 1936. It is called *Shirley Temple's Favorite Poems*. Although Shirley's name is on the cover, she is not included anywhere else in the book.

This *Shirley Temple Pastime Book* was published by Saalfield in 1935. It contains games and puzzles but the contents don't pertain to Shirley. Her picture appears on the cover and the inside page of the book.

These boxed books were published by Saalfield in 1936. The set includes five different books. The box is #1730 and is called *Five Books About Me*.

The Saalfield Co. produced a book called *Shirley Temple's Book of Fairy Tales* in 1936. The book was published exactly as it had been in 1922 except that Shirley's picture was added to the front cover and throughout the book to make another marketable Shirley Temple book.

This Shirley Temple stationary is marked "Copyrighted 1936 by W. T. and S. Corp." It has never been used.

The Shirley Temple doll trunks are made of wood with leather corners and handle. Decals of Shirley on the trunk identify it as an authentic Shirley trunk. Pictured is a trunk that would accommodate a 15″ tall doll. Shown with the trunk are homemade dresses made in the late 1930s for a 13″ tall Shirley Temple doll.

Shirley Temple doll buggies were also made in order for Shirley dolls to have transportation. This picture, promoting the dolls and buggies, comes from an early Shirley Temple scrapbook. The buggies were made in two styles. Besides wicker, another model was made of wood. Shirley's picture was on the buggy and her name was on the hubcaps. The buggies were made by the F. A. Whitney Carriage Co.

Even common school tablets sold better with a picture of Shirley on the cover. This one dates from the mid-thirties.

Out for a walk with her doll, Shirley Temple, 20th Century-Fox star, wears a dainty frock of light blue contrasted with inverted pleats of navy. The short puff sleeves scallop the two shades together

This scrapbook item pictures Shirley in one of her ads for Quaker Puffed Wheat. Shirley did not advertise products as often as the Dionne Quints, when she was a child, but she did endorse more products during her young adult years.

This blue depression glass pitcher was given as an advertising premium for two packages of Wheaties cereal in 1936. Consumers could also obtain a cereal bowl or a mug to go with the pitcher. The pitchers are currently being reproduced, but this one is old. The original glassware was made by Hazel Atlas Glass Co. This pitcher is from the collection of Stan Shivers.

This was one of a set of twelve pictures produced to advertise the Wheaties breakfast cereal. The photos came with the cereal boxes.

Wee Willie Winkie, one of Shirley's Fox films from 1937 was based on the story by Rudyard Kipling. Saalfield published this book as a tie-in to the new movie. Many movie scenes from the film were included in the book along with the plot of the picture.

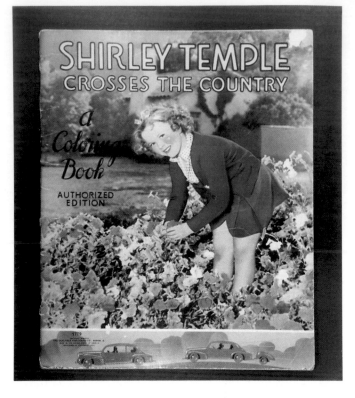

In 1937 Fox made a movie of the Johanni Spyri classic story *Heidi* with Shirley playing the title role. These tie-in books published by Saalfield make wonderful collectors' items since they list the cast members plus the plot and pictures from each of the films.

Shirley Temple Crosses the Country was the title of the coloring book published by Saalfield in 1939 to take advantage of the publicity given to the Temple's real trip across the country. It is #1779.

This postcard of Shirley Temple's home was mailed to the folks back home in Kansas City, Missouri during a vacation in California in 1938. Most of the tourists in those days made a bus tour to the movie star homes.

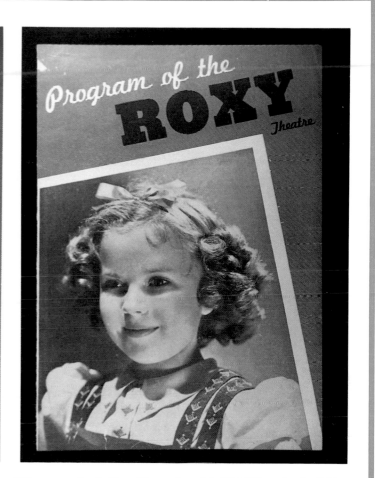

Sheet music called "An Old Straw Hat" from Shirley's Twentieth Century Fox film, *Rebecca of Sunnybrook Farm* from 1938. It was by Mack Gordon and Harry Revel and was published by Leo Feist, Inc.

This program for the Roxy Theater from July 29, 1938 was for the Shirley Twentieth Century-Fox film *Little Miss Broadway*. Her picture is on the cover.

Shirley's Fox film *Just Around the Corner* was playing at the Missouri Theater in Maryville, Missouri in December, 1938. Although Shirley was growing up, her films were still very popular.

In 1939 Shirley made her first film in color. It was called *The Little Princess* and can be seen on video cassette today as can many of the Temple pictures. A Shirley Temple coloring book was published in 1939 by Saalfield called *The Little Princess* to tie-in with this movie. The number is #1784. Her other Twentieth Century-Fox film for 1939 was *Susannah of the Mounties*. Although movie posters and lobby cards from Shirley's early films are very expensive, such material from her later movies is usually priced reasonably. Although Shirley's popularity was waning, she was selected to be Grand Marshall of the fiftieth Rose Parade in 1939.

In 1940, Shirley Temple made her last films for Fox. The movies were *The Blue Bird* and *Young People*. Shirley had outgrown her curls and little girl parts and was not quite ready for adolescent roles. She was at the "awkward age." Fox terminated her contract and Shirley had to adjust to a different life style. She had always been tutored on the set so she had not yet gone to a regular school. She enrolled in Westlake School for Girls as a seventh grader. Shirley thought she was only twelve years old, but she was really thirteen because the studio had moved her age back a year in order to maker her seem as young as possible.

Although her movie career did not remain idle for long, Shirley Temple was never again to resume her stature as the star she had been as a youngster. Metro-Goldwyn-Mayer signed her to a contract in 1940 for a salary of $100,000 a year. Her first film for M-G-M was *Kathleen* made in 1941. This began Shirley Temple's second career as she moved into teenage and adult movie roles.

A half sheet movie poster of *Honeymoon* which starred Shirley in 1946. The film was made for RKO.

Shirley made *Adventure in Baltimore* for RKO in 1949. This is a still showing Shirley with co-star Robert Young.

Shirley received third billing in this ad when she co-starred with Cary Grant and Myrna Loy in *The Bachelor and the Bobby-Soxer* hit RKO film in 1947.

Shirley was also used for the cover subject on *Modern Screen* for February, 1948.

Screen Stories from May, 1948 featured real life husband and wife John Agar and Shirley Temple on its cover in a scene from their new movie *Fort Apache* made by Argosy Pictures for RKO with John Wayne as its star.

Screen Guide for November, 1943 used Shirley as their cover art as she began making movies for Selznek.

Shirley's picture represented her birthday month of October on the 1950 calendar produced by *Motion Picture* magazine.

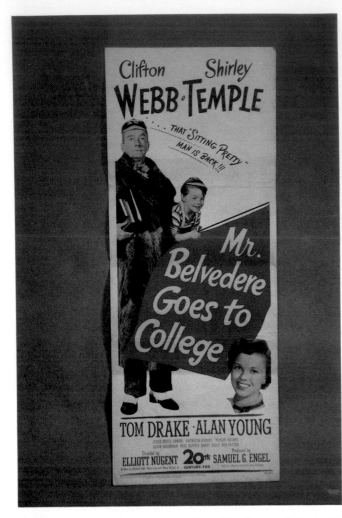

This insert is for the 1949 film *Mr. Belvedere Goes to College* which starred Clifton Webb and Shirley Temple. The movie was made by Twentieth Century Fox.

A lobby card from the film called *A Kiss for Corliss* which Shirley made in 1949. The film was released by United Artists.

Look magazine featured Shirley with her daughter Linda Susan on their cover for February 15, 1949. An article inside the magazine pictured Shirley, her husband, and their small daughter.

Shirley co-starred with Lon McCallister in the Warners film, *The Story of Seabiscuit* in 1949 her last year of film making.

"Watch Your Step, Lana!" Page 28

modern screen

august 15c

SHIRLEY TEMPLE
and
LINDA SUSAN

Modern Screen also featured Shirley with her daughter on their cover for August, 1948.

Their son, Charles, was born there in 1952. During their stay in Washington, Shirley met lots of government people and this was the first experience she had with diplomats and embassies. She became aware of a whole different world than any she had known before as she received an education on how government matters are handled.

At the end of the Korean War, the Blacks moved back to California. In 1954, Shirley's second daughter, Lori, was born. Besides raising her family, Shirley devoted much of her time to charity work in the state of California.

In 1957 Shirley Temple began her "third" show business career when she agreed to do the "Shirley Temple Storybook" series on television. Shirley acted as mistress of ceremonies on the program and also starred in some of the episodes. With the publicity generated by the series, the child Shirley Temple had been again captured the spotlight. Many products were produced to take advantage of this publicity. The Ideal Co. issued new Shirley Temple dolls, this time made of vinyl and plastic. The dolls were made in sizes of 12", 15", 17", 19" and 36". Because these dolls do not craze or crack, they can usually be found in very good condition. The dolls that are mint in the boxes are, of course, the most desirable. The most expensive of these dolls today is the 36" model. These "new" Shirley Temple dolls were still being advertised in 1962 in the Sears Christmas catalog. The 12" doll with four outfits and accessories was priced at $9.89 and a 15" doll dressed in a Heidi costume was priced at $6.98. The basic 12" doll in a slip sold for from $3.00-$4.00 during the late 1950s. Costumes for these dolls could also be sewed at home and several commercial patterns were manufactured to supply designs for clothing for the popular "new" Shirley Temple dolls.

Pictured are two 12" tall vinyl Shirley Temple dolls made in the late 1950s. One is wearing her original red cotton Shirley Temple dress and the other is dressed in her original slip, shoes and socks and still retains her tag. The dolls are marked on the back of the head "Ideal Doll / ST-12" and "ST—12N" on the shoulder. Both dolls have rooted saran hair and sleep eyes.

$6⁹⁸

$9⁸⁹

Famous Shirley Temple Dolls

Dimple-cheeked Shirley is sure to enchant your young actress. Doll is fashioned of nearly unbreakable plastic. She has jointed arms and legs; a soft vinyl plastic head that turns, with curly, rooted Saran hair that can be brushed, combed and even washed. Long lashes fringe her closing eyes.

15-inch Shirley dressed in "Heidi" costume —styled after her famous movie. Her glossy, rooted Saran hair is set in beautiful curls. Assorted style, colorful cotton dress is trimmed in ric-rac and embroidery. She also comes wearing pretty lace-edged undies, a pair of knit socks and vinyl shoes.
49 N 3628—Shpg. wt. 2 lbs. $6.98

12-inch Shirley with 4 outfits and accessories . . all in a pretty gift box. It's fun to dress her into so many different moods with the big wardrobe included. She's dressed in lacy rayon slip, panties, shoes, socks. Outfits consist of: tailored trench-coat, tote bag, hat; cotton gown, plastic purse; sun dress and sun glasses. For dress-up, she has a nylon party dress with sewed-in cotton slip and imitation pearl necklace. Outfits may vary slightly.
49 N 3986—Shipping weight 2 pounds 12 ounces...........$9.89

The *Sears Christmas Catalog* for 1962 was still featuring Shirley Temple dolls. The 12″ tall doll with four outfits was priced at $9.89 and the 15″ tall doll dressed as Heidi was $6.98.

Besides dolls, paper dolls were also designed to tie-in to the new television program. Most of the new sets were again made by Saalfield including *Shirley Temple Play Kit* #9859 in 1958, *Shirley Temple* #1320, and *Shirley Temple Dolls and Dresses* #1739 in 1959. Gabriel Sons and Co. also manufactured a *Magnetic Shirley Temple Doll* #303 and a *Shirley Temple Snap On* boxed paper doll set in 1958.

Coloring books also were produced to feature the "child" Shirley Temple. They included two by Saalfield numbered 4584 and 4624.

At this same time, books based on Shirley's old movies were also produced. The hardback books published by Random House all featured pictures of the young Shirley in scenes from her films. Titles included: *Heidi, Susannah of the Mounties, The Littlest Rebel, Rebecca, Captain January,* and *The Little Colonel,* with the last two both in one volume.

Although there were fewer products featuring the Storybook program itself, some toys were made. One of the items was a Shirley Temple Magnetic TV Theater by Amsco Toys made in 1959. Most of the products that were manufactured were books or records featuring Shirley telling stories for children.

Several unusual children's beauty sets were manufactured at this time with a Shirley endorsement. The Gabriel Company produced nine different Beauty-Aid sets including one called "Hair Styler."

This Simplicity doll pattern was printed in the late 1950s when the first vinyl Shirley Temple dolls were produced. The back of the pattern states it is for the Shirley Temple 19″ doll.

The *Shirley Temple Play Kit* produced by Saalfield in 1958. It is #9859. The $1.00 item included two paper dolls, lace on dresses, as well as a coloring book and crayons.

This unusual 18″ tall paper doll, made in two pieces, was published by Saalfield in 1959. The book is #1320.

Saalfield also produced coloring books of Shirley during the 1950s including this one, #4584, published in 1958. This book is especially nice because the inside pictures are also of Shirley.

Shirley Temple Dolls and Dresses was another paper doll set published by Saalfield in 1959. It contained two dolls and clothing, and was #1739.

This Shirley Temple coloring book was published by Saalfield in the late 1950s. It is #4624. It includes many pictures of Shirley inside the book.

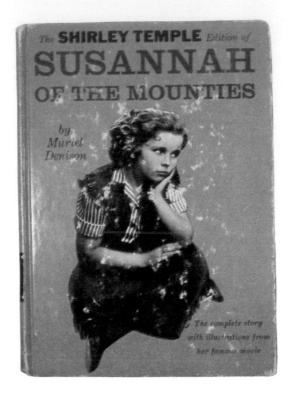

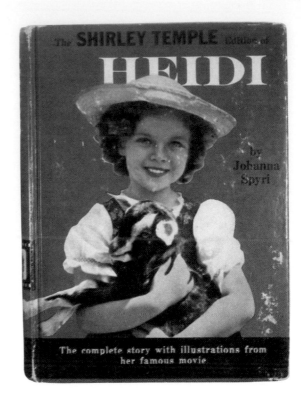

With the new interest in Shirley through her television series, earlier books were published again in new editions. Pictured is *Susannah of the Mounties* published by Random House in 1959. The story is by Muriel Denison but it is illustrated with pictures from Shirley's film. Also shown is the *Heidi* book from 1959. The story is by Johanna Spyri but the Random House book is illustrated with photos from Shirley's 1937 movie.

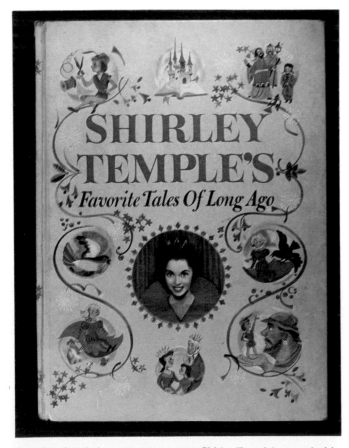

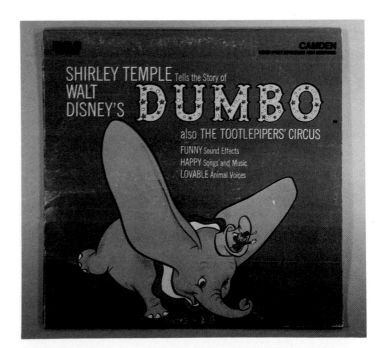

One of the few tie-ins to actually promote Shirley Temple's new television series is this book called *Shirley Temple's Favorite Tales of Long Ago*. It was published by Random House in 1958. Pictures of Shirley are included on the front and back cover.

Records were also produced to tie-in to Shirley's television show. This one is by RCA Records and is called *Shirley Temple Tells the Story of Walt Disney's Dumbo*. Shirley is the narrator. It was made in 1960.

Gabriel Industries, Inc. produced several different little girl's beauty products with a Shirley Temple endorsement in the late 1950s. Pictured is one called *Hair Styler* which includes shampoo, creme rinse, and hair dressing. Other sets were called, *Glamour Girl*, *Beauty Bar*, *Manicure Set*, and *Fresh-Up Kit*.

"Shirley Temple's Storybook" was on NBC from January until September, 1958 and then was shown on ABC from January to June, 1959. Finally it was returned to NBC as "The Shirley Temple Show" from September, 1960 until it finished its run in September, 1961.

While still working on the television program, Shirley Temple began her active role in politics in 1960 when she helped with the Richard Nixon presidential campaign. In 1964 she also campaigned for Republican Barry Goldwater in his presidential try. With this experience behind her, Shirley decided to try for political office herself. In 1967 she ran an unsuccessful campaign for Congress as a Republican.

In 1968 Shirley Temple again campaigned for Nixon as he sought another term as president. After his election he appointed his supporter to be a U. S. delegate to the United Nations. After Shirley successfully fulfilled this obligation, President Ford recognized her contribution by naming her as the Ambassador to Ghana in Africa. With the completion of Shirley's ambassadorship, she was appointed as Chief of Protocol in Washington. Shirley Temple Black has continued her successful government work and was assigned to be Ambassador to Czechoslovakia in 1989. This job was especially rewarding to the former child star as she had been in Czechoslovakia in 1968 when the country fell to the communists.

Even though Shirley Temple Black has become a respected diplomat, fans have not forgotten the child star she once was. Toys in her image continue to be re-issued to take advantage of this fame. A new style Shirley Temple doll was produced by the Ideal Co. in 1973. The doll has rooted hair, painted eyes, is 16" tall, and is made of vinyl. To help celebrate its anniversary, the Montgomery Ward Co. featured a slightly different version of the vinyl Shirley Temple in its catalog in 1972. Two new sets of Shirley Temple paper dolls were also produced in the 1970s by the Whitman Publishing Co.

Pictured are items from Shirley Temple Black's unsuccessful 1967 campaign for the California 11th district Congressional seat. She ran as a Republican. From the collection of Marge Meisinger.

199

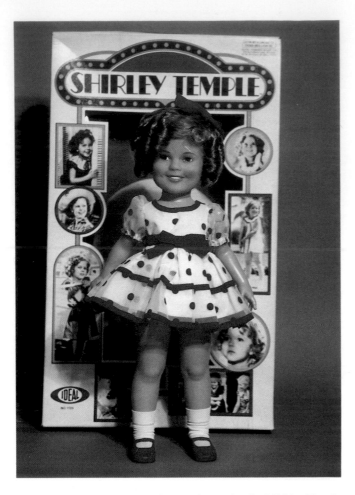

Whitman Publishing Co. produced a boxed set of Shirley Temple paper dolls in 1976. One heavy doll and clothing to be punched out were included in the set.

In 1973, the Ideal Company again manufactured a vinyl Shirley Temple doll. She is 16″ tall with painted features and rooted hair. She is shown with her original box and clothing.

Whitman Publishing Co. secured the rights to Shirley Temple products in the 1970s and the firm produced this paper doll book in 1976. There was only one doll in the book along with punch out clothing. The number is 1986.

In 1982, 1983 and 1984 new lines of Shirley dolls were introduced to the American public. Ideal again made the vinyl dolls in 1982 and 1983 but they did not sell as well as earlier models. The dolls produced in 1984 included a large 36″ model of Shirley and a vinyl Baby Shirley Temple doll. The later dolls were expensive and were made primarily for collectors and not as toys for children as all the other Shirley dolls had been.

In 1989 Shirley Temple Black was again asked to be the Grand Marshall of the *Tournament of Roses Parade* in Pasadena to celebrate the 50th anniversary of her 1939 Rose Parade appearance and the 100th anniversary of the parade itself. Perhaps the adult Mrs. Black and the child Shirley have merged at last.

The most loved piece in a Shirley Temple collection may be an autographed picture of Shirley herself. It reminds us all of the successful adult life achieved by this child star of the 1930s. Most of Shirley's contemporaries grew up to face problems they could not overcome while Shirley Temple Black has continued to grow and succeed as an adult. No wonder Shirley Temple collectors continue to multiply. These collectors pay homage to an admirable woman as well as to a delightful child of the past.

For interested collectors:

The Shirley Temple Collectors News
8811 Colonial Road
Brooklyn, NY 11209
Rita Dubas, Publisher
$20 per year for four issues
Includes ads for Shirley Collectibles

In 1982, the Ideal Company again re-issued several different vinyl Shirley Temple dolls. Pictured here is an 8″ doll dressed as The Little Colonel and a 12″ doll model dressed in a Captain January costume. Many different costumes were made for the different models of these dolls. They have sleep eyes and rooted hair.

In 1989 Shirley Temple was again asked to be the Grand Marshall of the *Tournament Of Roses Parade*. The parade marked the 100th anniversary of the celebration and since Shirley had been the Marshall on the parade's 50th anniversary she was asked to repeat her success by heading the 100th Rose Parade. Pictured is the cover of the program. The program for 1939 cost 10 cents and the one from 1989 was $4.00. From the collection of Marge Meisinger.

Most fans appreciate a Shirley Temple autograph as much as anything in their collections. Although early Shirley Temple signatures are hard to find, Shirley Temple Black is still generous in signing pictures for her fans.

John Wayne
The Duke

Movie still showing a young John Wayne as he looked in his early Western films.

John Wayne, the personification of American masculinity, was born with the rather feminine name of Marion Michael Morrison in Winterset, Iowa in 1907. His parents were Mary Brown Morrison (born in Ireland) and Clyde Morrison, a druggist. The family was complete when Robert was born a year later.

When Marion was only seven, the family left Iowa for California because Mr. Morrison suffered lung problems. They settled on a ninety acre homestead farm near Palmdale and lived in a small cabin Mr. Morrison built. The farm was not successful and after two years, the family moved to Glendale where Mr. Morrison found work in a drugstore.

Although his parents still called Marion by his given name, he secured the nickname "Duke" while he lived in Glendale because

of a dog he owned whose name was Duke. For fun, Marion and the neighborhood gang loved to watch movies being made at the Triangle studios in Glendale. This love of films also made Duke a Saturday matinee movie fan at the local theater. A newspaper route provided the funds to continue this interest for the youngster.

Marion was a good student and athlete in high school and after graduation he received a football scholarship to attend the University of Southern California. He didn't complete college, however, for a football injury made it impossible for him to return to active sports participation and he couldn't afford to attend school without the football scholarship.

With the help of his coach and movie star Tom Mix, a summer job was arranged for Duke as a prop man for Fox. Wayne decided to keep the job year round when he wasn't able to return to the University. John Ford also helped Wayne begin his career by getting him bit parts in several Fox movies, including *Hangman's House* in 1928.

Duke got a big break in his film career in 1930 when Raoul Walsh gave him the lead in *The Big Trail*. Even with his name changed to John Wayne, the movie was still a flop. Because of the way it was filmed, special equipment was needed to show the film and not many theaters were equipped to book it.

Wayne then signed with Columbia and appeared in several small roles in the studio's movies before being dropped in 1932. For the next eight years he worked for Monogram, Republic, and Universal doing lots of cheap Western films. With steady work and an income of around $150 per week, Wayne could afford to marry his long-time girl friend, Josie Saenz. Her father was a Panamanian envoy serving in the consulate at Los Angeles and the couple had met while Marion was still in college. Although Josie came from a wealthy background and Wayne's early life had sometimes been spent in near poverty, the two had been in love for some time. The couple remained married for over ten years- divorcing in 1944 after a family of four children had been born to them: Michael in 1934, Toni in 1936, Patrick in 1938, and Melinda in 1940.

In 1936, John Wayne received a new picture deal with Universal. He was to make eight films and would receive $6,000 for each one. That was more money than he had ever made before.

By 1938 John Wayne had been making movies for ten years and had appeared in at least sixty-two pictures. He still was not known to the general movie-going public. That would change in 1939.

In that year, his old friend John Ford got him his first really good role as the Ringo Kid in the film *Stagecoach*. The picture was made for United Artists and it was a big hit. Although Wayne did well in the part and movie magazines took notice of him for the

John Wayne's first big hit movie was *Stagecoach* made for United Artists in 1939. This ad appeared in *Hollywood* magazine March, 1939.

A Lady Takes a Chance with Jean Arthur as Wayne's co-star was made by RKO in 1943. This ad appeared in *Screen Guide* November, 1943.

first time, he still did not become a big star. He was under contract to Republic Studios at that time. The studio was started in 1935 and it specialized in low budget westerns. Wayne was paid only $200 per week even when he was borrowed by other studios to make pictures for them. His next film to receive critical acclaim was made in 1940 for United Artists with John Ford again as director. It was called *The Long Voyage Home* and was based on a one-act play by Eugene O'Neill. The movie is still considered to be one of John Wayne's best.

With the coming of World War II, Wayne's career gained momentum. As the father of four children he was exempt from the draft and since there were not too many "he men" Hollywood personalities available, Wayne was borrowed by several other studios to play male leads. He was cast in *Reap the Wild Wind* for Paramount in 1942, with Paulette Goddard as his co-star, and in *The Spoilers* for Universal, also in 1942, with Marlene Dietrich.

At his home studio, Republic, he made his first World War II movie that same year. It was called *The Flying Tigers* and it proved to be a popular picture. The film still draws a good audience when it is shown on television today.

In 1943 RKO borrowed Wayne to play opposite Jean Arthur in *A Lady Takes a Chance*. Since this film was for a well-established studio, *Screen Guide* did a two page picture spread on the movie in its August, 1943 issue. The film was also widely advertised in the movie magazines of the period. With his home studio, Wayne also made a film called *In Old Oklahoma* the same year. Martha Scott co-starred.

With the success of *The Flying Tigers*, John Wayne made another World War II film for Republic in 1944. It was called *The Fighting Seabees*. RKO borrowed Wayne again in 1944 to make a comedy with Ella Raines called *Tall in the Saddle*. Although the film isn't too well-remembered today, it was a popular movie in 1944.

Sheet music from the John Wayne Republic picture *In Old Oklahoma* made in 1943. The song is "Put Your Arms Around Me Honey" by Junie McCree and Albert Von Tilzer. It was published by Broadway Music Corp.

In 1945, Wayne made two more successful war movies. One titled *Back to Bataan* was made for RKO and the other film was an M-G-M movie called *They Were Expendable*. Robert Montgomery was his co-star.

After Wayne's divorce from Josie, he married another Latin girl in 1946. She was a Mexican actress named Esperanza Bauer. The seven-year marriage between the two was often stormy and resulted in a bitter divorce with full newspaper coverage.

John Wayne continued to work regularly after World War II but he still had not reached the star status that eventually would be his. Although fan magazines did include Wayne's pictures in their issues, and scrapbooks of the 1940s usually contained some Wayne portraits, there were not nearly as many pictures of Wayne as of stars like Clark Gable or Gary Cooper. In 1946, he continued the practice of being loaned to other studios when he made a film called *Without Reservations* for RKO, which co-starred Claudette Colbert.

In 1947 John Wayne returned to his home studio when he made a picture called *Angel and the Badman* for Republic with Gail Russell. Gail's name would later come up in the Wayne divorce action when charges were being made by both parties as to their mate's misbehavior.

They Were Expendable was another Wayne war picture made by M-G-M in 1945.

Movie Stars Parade for April, 1947 featured an ad for the John Wayne—Gail Russell Republic film, *Angel and the Badman*. A personal relationship between the co-stars would make the news several years later during John Wayne's divorce trial.

Wayne continued to advance his career with the help of successful war movies during World War II. *Back to Bataan* was made for RKO in 1945. This ad was carried by *Screen Stars* September, 1945.

Although John Wayne was the star of *Fort Apache* (United Artists), 1948, he was overshadowed in the publicity for the movie by his fellow players, Shirley Temple and her husband John Agar acting in their only film together. *Screen Stories* magazine for May, 1948 did a story with pictures on the movie, but most of the coverage went to the two young actors. Other magazines also carried advertising material for the popular film.

Wayne fared better in his other United Artists film for 1948. It was called *Red River* and the movie was his biggest commercial success up to that time. It was directed by Howard Hawks and co-starred Montgomery Clift. Critics consider the film one of Wayne's ten best pictures.

With another successful film called *She Wore a Yellow Ribbon* in 1949, John Wayne, for the first time, made it to the list of the ten top box office stars, placing fourth. This film contained what John Wayne said was his favorite role. John Ford was again his director and the film was made by RKO.

In 1950 with the release of *Sands of Iwo Jima* and *Rio Grande*, both made by Republic, Wayne became the number one box office star in the country. He repeated the feat in 1951 making three films for three different studios: *Operation Pacific* (Warners), *The Bullfighter and the Lady* (Republic) and *Flying Leathernecks* (RKO).

All through the 1950s, John Wayne continued to make good films. One of his best was *The Quiet Man* (Republic) in 1952. This movie turned out to be the biggest hit Republic Studios ever had. His co-star was Maureen O'Hara. The same year, Wayne was also still making small budget films for Republic including *Big Jim McLain* which is largely forgotten today.

One of John Wayne's best films was made in 1948 for United Artists and was advertised in *Photoplay* magazine October, 1948. The film was *Red River* co-starring Montgomery Clift.

In 1948, *Fort Apache* was considered such a big film that a large two page ad was carried in the *Saturday Evening Post* for March 20, 1948. The film was an Argosy Picture released through RKO. Henry Fonda, Shirley Temple, and her husband, John Agar were also in the movie along with John Wayne.

A lobby card from *The Quiet Man*, Republic's big John Wayne hit from 1952. Maureen O'Hara was the co-star.

After a long career at Republic, John Wayne signed with Warner Brothers and in 1956 he became the highest paid actor in the world when he made $666,666.

Other successful Wayne films from the 1950s include: *Island in the Sky* (1953); *The High and the Mighty* (1954); *The Searchers* (1956); and *Rio Bravo* (1959). All of these movies were made by Warner Brothers. Wayne also starred in a very unlikely film in the 1950s when he played Genghis Khan in the movie called *The Conqueror*. Even popular co-star Susan Hayworth couldn't help John Wayne in this miscast role. The film was featured in one of Dell Publishing Co.'s Movie Classic comics.

In 1954 Wayne married his third and last wife, Pilar Palette (Mrs. Dick Weldy). Pilar had been a minor actress in Peru but had not attempted to further her career after her first marriage. She and Wayne became parents to the last of the Wayne children: Assa in 1956, John in 1962, and Marisa in 1966.

Although John Wayne's image was not used on as many products as other western stars like Roy Rogers and Gene Autry, toys were made to honor Wayne's stature as a popular western star. A coloring book was published by Saalfield in 1951 which featured both biographical and movie-related pictures to color. It is a scarce item. Another interesting Wayne collectible is a jigsaw puzzle that was produced in 1951.

John Wayne advertising collectibles are also more scarce than those for other Western stars but the Wayne image was used on several products, usually in conjunction with the promotion of an upcoming movie. The Dixie ice cream lid is one such product. Many star photographs were used on the lids to tie-in with new films. These lids could then be collected and exchanged for larger star photographs made in color.

In 1960, John Wayne decided to film a favorite historical event when he began producing, directing and starring in *The Alamo*, the story of Davy Crockett and his fellow Americans' fight to win

In 1953 Wayne made *Island in the Sky* for Warner Brothers. Shown is a lobby card from this film.

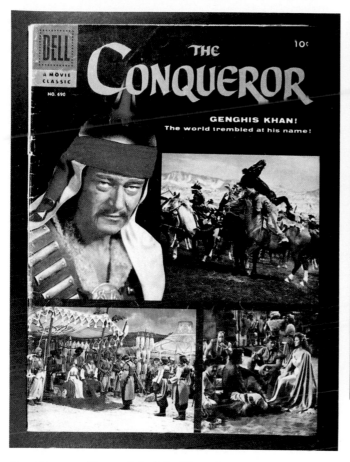

One of the worst films made by John Wayne is represented by this Movie Classic comic book published by Dell Publishing in 1956. It is based on the film *The Conqueror* made for RKO in which Wayne played Genghis Khan.

Saalfield Publishing Co. produced this John Wayne puzzle in 1951. It makes a nice collectible for Wayne fans.

This Dixie ice cream lid advertises Nelson's Cloverland Ice Cream by using a picture of John Wayne starring in *The Quiet Man* in 1952. The advertising encourages fans to save lids to turn in to the company in exchange for a colored picture of John Wayne. Many other star photos were also used on Dixie cup lids.

Texas from Mexico. The picture went way over budget and Wayne had to mortgage nearly everything to get it finished. The movie, which eventually cost over twelve million dollars, was not a success at the box office. With so much of his own money in the film, it took Wayne years to work his way back to financial security.

Besides the expensive "Alamo" Wayne made a film for Twentieth Century-Fox in 1960 called *North To Alaska*. Dell Movie Classics also produced a comic book of that Wayne movie.

John Wayne continued his astonishing movie career in the 1960s with more hit films including: *The Comancheros* (Twentieth Century-Fox, 1961); *The Man Who Shot Liberty Valance* (Paramount, 1962); *How the West Was Won* (M-G-M, 1964); and *Hatari!* (Paramount, 1962); *The Longest Day* (Twentieth Century-Fox, 1963); *Donovan's Reef* (Paramount, 1963); and *McLintock* (United Artists, 1963).

Although John Wayne continued to make films regularly, his health made the next big news. After suffering with a cough for some time, he checked into Hollywood's Good Samaritan Hospital in September, 1964. Wayne then had surgery to remove part of a lung, and was diagnosed as having had cancer. Wayne made his surgery public in order to encourage others to seek treatment if they suspected they, too, might have cancer.

By February, 1965, Wayne was ready to go back to work on his next film, *The Sons of Katie Elder*. He was fifty-eight years old, had made at least 138 movies and had licked the "Big C" as he called it. *Life* magazine did a cover story on his recovery in their May 7, 1965 issue and also included pictures of him working on his new movie.

John Wayne produced, directed and starred in the film, *The Alamo* in 1960. This record contains the original sound track recording from the film and was made by Columbia. The music was composed and conducted by Dimitri Tiomkin and the lyrics were by Paul Francis Webster.

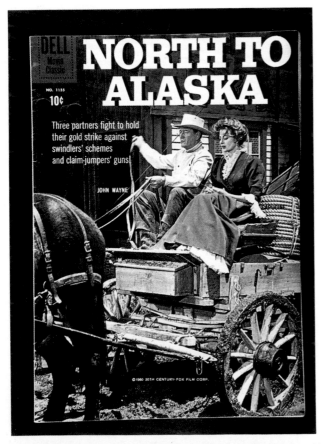

Pictured is a commercial program for the John Wayne Paramount film, *Hatari!* made in 1962. The book included the plot of the movie as well as many pictures of the cast and the crew during the making of the film.

Dell Publishing Co. produced this Movie Classic comic *North to Alaska* in 1960 to tie-in with the John Wayne film made for Twentieth Century-Fox. Stewart Granger, Ernie Kovacs and Capucine were also in the movie.

A still of John Wayne from the 1965 Paramount film, *The Sons of Katie Elder*. It was the first movie the star made after his cancer surgery in 1964.

As John Wayne got older, he seemed to become more conservative. He had aligned himself on the side of the people hunting out communist sympathizers in the 1950s and in the late 1960s he cast his lot with those Americans who supported the war in Vietnam. In order to publicize his beliefs, he made a film for Warners in 1968 called *The Green Berets*. Because there was so much opposition to the war by so many people, it is surprising that the film became such a hit. It grossed over eleven million dollars despite poor critical reception by most reviewers.

Other fine John Wayne films from the 1960s included: *In Harms Way* (Paramount, in 1965); *El Dorado* (Paramount, 1967); and of course, *True Grit* (Paramount in 1969). In *True Grit*, Wayne played Rooster Cogburn, a gunfighter with only one eye who wore a black eye patch. *Time* magazine featured Wayne on its August 8, 1969 cover in this role. John Wayne continued to be among the top box office stars of the country just as he had been twenty years earlier in his long career. He also received his only Academy Award for best actor that year for his Rooster Cogburn performance. Besides being the most popular star of sound films ever, he had now been acknowledged as a fine actor by his peers.

John Wayne made several more good movies in the 1970s including *Rio Lobo* (National General, in 1971); *The Cowboys* (Warner Brothers, in 1972); and perhaps his best of the 1970s and his last film *The Shootist* (Dino De Laurentis, 1976). His last movie, appropriately, was about a gunfighter who was dying of cancer.

John Wayne's health again became a topic of concern in 1978 when he had open heart surgery in April of that year at the age of seventy. He seemed to make a good recovery, but when he returned to the hospital for a gall stone operation in January, 1979, the doctors found cancer in his stomach. John Wayne lost this second battle with the "Big C" on June 11, 1979.

John Wayne made over 150 films during his fifty year career. There were only a few years from 1949 until 1974 when John Wayne wasn't one of the top ten box office movie stars. He had been in first place five times and in second place three times. His name had been included in the top five stars twenty-three times by the end of his career. He is the biggest money maker in film history and his movies have made over $700 million in the last fifty years.

John Wayne films are still seen daily on television stations all over the country. Fans particularly enjoy his war and western roles. John Wayne was a large man; six feet four inches tall and weighing over two hundred pounds. His leathery, weather-beaten look and his tough manner were perfect for these films.

More than ten years after his death, products are still being produced in Wayne's image. Recent paper dolls featured costumes from some of Wayne's most remembered movie roles. The paper dolls were drawn by Tom Tierney. A doll made by the Effanbee Doll Corp., as one of its Legend Series of dolls in 1981, is dressed in a copy of one of John Wayne's western costumes. Both items provide unusual keepsakes for John Wayne collectors.

John Wayne, the most popular hero of sound films, will be remembered as he was on the screen. The Western star was a man bigger than life, who gave movie fans a few hours when they, too, could identify with a hero fighting off the villains and, at least in the fantasy world of films, making sure the good guys won.

The birthplace of John Wayne is maintained as a museum at 224 South Second Street, Winterset, Iowa 50273

For interested fans:

The Big Trail: A Newsletter of the Films of John Wayne
540 Stanton Ave.
Akron, OH 44301

$11.00 per year for six issues
Includes ads for buying and selling
Tim Lilley, Ed.

A book called *John Wayne Paper Dolls* published by Dover Publishers in 1981. Tom Tierney is the artist and he includes many of the costumes from the hit John Wayne films.

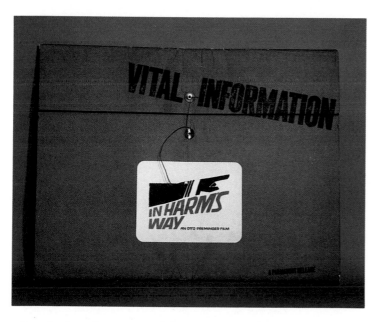

Press book made to promote Wayne's 1965 film *In Harm's Way*. The picture was made for Paramount and co-starred Kirk Douglas.

This John Wayne vinyl doll was made by the Effanbee Doll Corp. as one of its Legend Series of dolls in 1981. He is dressed in a western costume.

John Wayne will be remembered in "he man" roles like *Big Jake*, which he made in 1971. Richard Boone and Maureen O'Hara were co-stars in the movie made for Cinema Center Films.

Jane Withers

The Movie Brat

A still of the young child star, Jane Withers, when she worked at Twentieth Century-Fox.

The 1930s have given us some of the most memorable movie stars of all time. Major stars like Clark Gable, Katharine Hepburn, Cary Grant and Bette Davis began long-lasting careers that established them as popular screen artists for generations. This period of movies also spawned many lesser known Hollywood stars whose careers are valued more highly by collectors than by movie critics.

Such a player is Jane Withers. She came to Hollywood during a period that proved to be the heyday for young actors. Shirley Temple's phenomenal impact had made every stage mother dream of her own child striking it lucky in Hollywood. Every studio developed its own stable of child actors and some of them were very good. The best of the crop included: Judy Garland, Shirley Temple, Mickey Rooney, Freddie Bartholemew, Jackie Cooper, Deanna Durbin, and Jane Withers. These young people worked,

played, and went to school together at their various studios. At the same time these children earned their film companies "big bucks," for in the depressing days of the 1930s a child's presence could offer a bright spot in an otherwise dull movie.

Jane Withers was born in Atlanta, Georgia in 1926 and was already an experienced radio performer when she reached Hollywood five years later. Her Atlanta weekly radio program was called "Aunt Sally's Kiddy Club" and the children sang, did imitations and acted in skits to entertain the radio audience.

Things weren't too easy for Jane and her mother when they first arrived in Hollywood. She secured a small part in a film called *Handle With Care* in 1933 and outside of a few extra calls, Jane's career was soon stalled. Mrs. Withers didn't give up. She enrolled her six-year old daughter in the Lawlor Professional School where Jane studied singing and dancing in addition to her regular class work.

Then Jane turned to radio again. She had been a winner in Atlanta radio and she also became successful on a children's radio show in Los Angeles. The program gave her the break she needed. When Fox was looking for a child to play opposite their darling Shirley Temple in *Bright Eyes*, someone remembered the little girl from the radio program and Jane was picked for the part. She was eight years old when she took her second shot at screen stardom. The contrast between the light, sweet, dimpled Shirley Temple and the dark, mean, sassy Jane Withers was great. The public loved Jane's performance and wanted to see more of her.

Jane began making movies as fast as she could, developing her tomboy character in film after film. She starred in *Ginger, This is the Life, Paddy O'Day, Gentle Julia, Little Miss Nobody, Pepper, The Farmer Takes a Wife* and *Can This Be Dixie?*, and she was still only nine years old.

By 1937 when she made the film, *Angel's Holiday*, she was earning $2,000 per week and was known as the "screen brat." Also in 1937, she was included among the top ten box office stars of Hollywood when she was listed in sixth place. By 1938 she had fallen to eighth place, but was still among the top ten. Jane knew her place in Hollywood was secure when her Westwood home was included as one of the postcards in the folder called *Home of the Movie Stars*.

As Jane's popularity grew so did the tie-in products made to take advantage of her success. The Madame Alexander Doll Co. produced a composition doll in 1937 called "Jane Withers." The doll was made in two different styles. The smaller 13″ model has a closed mouth while the larger 16″ and 21″ dolls have open mouths with teeth. These dolls, along with the Ideal Company's Judy Garland dolls, are the most sought after personality dolls in today's market.

A half sheet movie poster for the film, *This is the Life* starring Jane Withers made for Twentieth Century-Fox in 1935.

In 1937, Jane made a movie for Twentieth Century-Fox called *Angel's Holiday*. This is a lobby card from the picture.

The Longshaw Card Co. manufactured the folder called *Homes of the Movie Stars* in the 1930s. Pictured is a postcard of Jane Withers' home from the folder plus another card showing her house after a second floor was added.

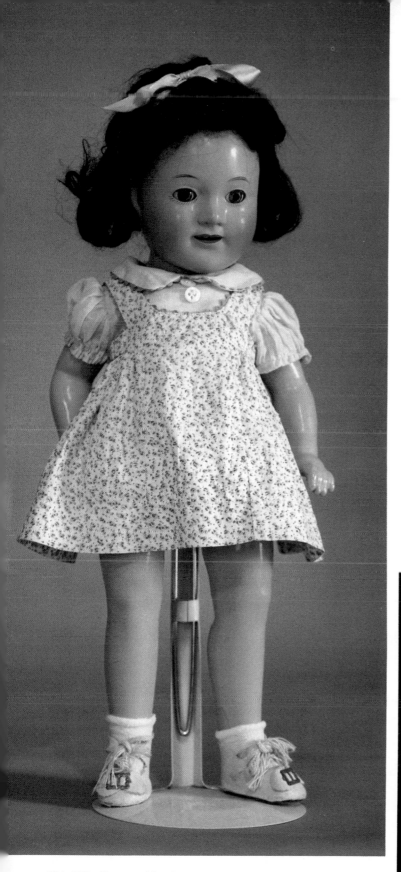

The print toy medium was also involved in promoting Jane Withers products. A song book called *Let's Sing Jane Withers Songs* was published by Movietone Music Corp. in 1938. The book contained pictures of Jane in movie costumes as well as songs from her films. Another book called *Jane Withers, Her Life Story* was published by the Whitman Publishing Co. in 1936. It also contains many pictures of the young star both at work and at home.

The Whitman Co. also had the authorization to publish paper dolls made in the likeness of the young star and they produced three books in the 1930s. The first called *Jane Withers*, was numbered 977 and featured a very large doll that was made in two pieces. The 1938 Whitman book was numbered 996 and featured two nice cutouts of Jane. A final book for 1938 was labeled by both the Dell Publishing Co. and the Whitman Co. and it featured two cutout dolls of Jane along with her clothing.

With the interest shown by fans, magazines began featuring articles and photos of Jane, and some even used her pictures as their cover pieces. Fans began clipping these pictures of the young Jane and many scrapbooks from the era can be found containing her pictures intermingled with those of Shirley Temple and the famous Dionne Quintuplets.

During the 1930s, in addition to giving away dishes, many movie theaters gave away free pictures of the stars to entice patrons to attend the movies. The backs of these photographs could be used to advertise future attractions. On the back of Jane's picture is an ad which promoted a Withers' movie called *45 Fathers*. The other advertising on the bill is interesting to read. The theater featured a bargain week where all admissions were two-for-one so two people could attend the movie for a quarter and children paid only a dime. Because Saturday was the big night for the movie in small town America the price was raised to 20 cents for adults but remained 10 cents for children. The advertising comes from Mound City, Missouri.

This 15″ tall composition Jane Withers doll was made by the Madame Alexander Doll Co. in 1937. The doll has a mohair wig, sleep eyes, and an open mouth with teeth. The doll is marked on the back, "Jane Withers/Alexander Doll." She is wearing her original dress.

This picture book called *Jane Withers: Her Life Story*, was published in 1936 by the Whitman Publishing Co.

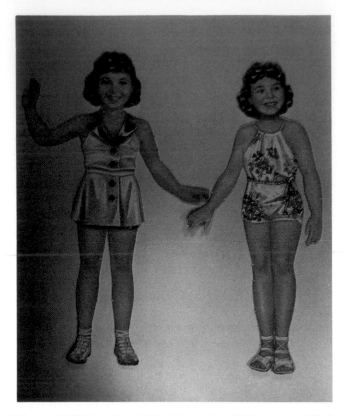

Whitman Publishing Co. published these Jane Withers paper dolls in 1938. The book was called *Jane Withers Cut-out Book* #996. Two dolls and clothing were featured.

The *Philadelphia Inquirer Picture Parade* for January 16, 1938 also featured a cover picture of Jane.

Silver Screen for June, 1938 used a cover photograph of Jane Withers.

A movie theater in Mound City, Missouri gave away this picture of Jane in the 1930s to promote the Withers movie called *45 Fathers*.

214

Although Jane Withers has been generous to her fans in supplying her autograph when requested to do so, her signature given as a child is not as easy to obtain. A large 11″ by 14″ picture of Jane signed for a studio wardrobe woman in 1939 is shown here.

Unlike most of the child stars of the 1930s, Jane Withers was able to continue her film career for thirteen years through adolescence into young adulthood. Because her career really was in two stages, child and young adult, there were many products produced to chronicle her child star years, then updated to reflect her teenage years. A coloring book called *Jane Withers* No. 607 was published by the Whitman Publishing Co. in 1941 when Jane was fifteen years old. A movie theater in Kansas City, Kansas also included Jane's photograph in a promotion give-away in the same year.

New sets of paper dolls were also being manufactured at this time to take advantage of Jane's new teenage image. The *Jane Withers Cut Out Book* was numbered 989 and was manufactured by the Whitman Co. It had one large doll and clothes and was produced in 1940. The last set of these Whitman paper dolls was published in 1941 and featured one smaller doll with lots of grown up clothing. It is numbered 986. All of these Jane Withers cut out books are in demand by paper doll collectors. As a result, movie buffs will have a hard time finding one in uncut condition.

The Whitman Publishing Co. also included Jane in their series of books from the 1940s when they used a fiction story and put a movie star on the cover and in drawings inside the book to give the books more selling power. They are now collector items. One of the books about Jane was titled, *Jane Withers and the Hidden Room*, published in 1943.

This coloring book called *Jane Withers* (#607) was published by the Whitman Publishing Co. in 1941 when Jane was fifteen years old.

Jane autographed this 11″ by 14″ picture for a studio worker in 1939.

A promotion booklet used by the Midway Theater in Kansas City, Missouri in 1941. The booklet was supplied to patrons and each week a Hollywood star photo was given away to be glued into the booklet. Shown are the pictures of Jane and Shirley Temple. Other stars also included were Clark Gable, Bing Crosby, Errol Flynn, and Mickey Rooney.

This set of Jane Withers paper dolls included only one large doll and clothing. It was produced in 1940 by the Whitman Publishing Co.

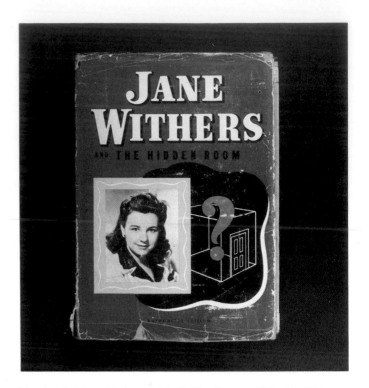

A book called *Jane Withers and the Hidden Room* published by Whitman Pub. Co. in 1942. Another book was published by the same company in 1943 called *Jane Withers and the Phantom Violin*.

This was the last set of commercial paper dolls made of Jane Withers by Whitman in 1941. The book had one doll and lots of adult clothing. The number is 986.

Because of the many movies Miss Withers appeared in, movie advertising material is fairly easy to obtain at reasonable prices. This is especially true of her later films such as *Chicken Wagon Family* produced in 1939 when Jane was still a star at Twentieth Century Fox.

As Jane Withers grew up, the fan magazine writers tried to treat her as if she was just another normal American teenager. Their stories concentrated on her interest in phonograph records (she had over 500), parties, Harry James, and boys. Photographers were invited to many of the young Hollywood stars' parties so the teenagers could be featured in the fan magazines.

In the meantime, for the most part, the Withers' films had deteriorated to "B" type pictures like *A Very Young Lady* from 1941. Most of the "B" pictures have been forgotten with one exception. It was the picture, *The North Star*, made for RKO in 1943. *The North Star* was a propaganda war film made to invoke sympathy for our Russian Allies during World War II. The film's creators were called before the House Un-American Activities Committee during the McCarthy era of the 1950s and questioned about the film's making. Along with Jane, Farley Granger, Anne Baxter, and Walter Huston were in the cast. Lillian Hellman wrote the script. Other later Withers' pictures of note included: *High School*, *Johnny Doughboy*, *Her First Beau*, *Golden Hoofs* (a horse story with Charles "Buddy" Rogers made in 1941), and *Faces in the Fog* from 1944.

In 1947 Jane Withers gave up the movies and married William Moss from Big Springs, Texas. They had three children (Wendy, William, and Randy) before they were divorced in 1954. In 1955 she married Kenneth Errair and both a son and a daughter were born to them before Errair was killed in a plane crash in 1968.

Miss Withers returned to Hollywood in 1956 when she played a very good character part in the blockbuster film, *Giant* made by Warner Brothers.

Jane Withers then turned to television commercials for her most lasting fame when she played the plumber Josephine. In this role she promoted Comet Cleanser for seventeen years.

Presently, the former child star, now a grandmother, keeps busy with promotional work at movie and doll conventions. Her fans are always happy to visit with the former "screen brat." Jane hopes to someday establish a museum to house her extensive doll collection. The collection began with dolls sent to the young star by fans and Miss Withers has continued to add to the collection as an adult.

Although she will never be considered a major star, Jane Withers did appear in around thirty movies over a period of thirteen years (not counting the later *Giant* years). While Jane's films were not always of the highest quality, the movies did allow a family of four to forget the depression for a few hours and attend a showing of *45 Fathers* in small towns like Mound City, Missouri for a cost of less than fifty cents. The memories of those family experiences are what make Jane Withers' career memorable.

A lobby card for the Jane Withers Twentieth Century-Fox film from 1941 called *A Very Young Lady*.

This *Chicken Wagon Family* movie poster was made for the Withers movie in 1939. The film was a Twentieth Century-Fox production.

In 1939 Jane made a forgettable movie called *High School* for Twentieth Century-Fox. A lobby card from the film is pictured here.

Jane was still making movies in the early 1940s but most of them were "B" pictures like this one called *Golden Hoofs* made by Twentieth Century-Fox in 1941. A lobby card from the movie pictures Jane in her role along with co-star Buddy Rogers.

The *Screen Romances* magazine for December, 1944 featured the Withers movie *Faces in the Fog* in story and pictures. Republic Pictures was responsible for the film.

One of Jane's most famous roles was that of Josephine, the plumber for Comet Cleanser. The ads were also used in the print medium. This one is from *McCall's* magazine for December, 1967.

Suggested Sources for Movie Memorabilia

ACS
1770 N. Highland Ave. #434
Hollywood, CA 90028
Master Celebrity Address List
Of over 7,000 personalities for $20

The Antique Trader
P.O. Box 1050
Dubuque, IA 52001
Weekly publication $24.00
Price Guide, six times a year $12

Bob Bennett Autographs
One Governor's Lane
Shelburne, VT 05482
Dealer in movie star autographs and author of *A Collectors' Guide to Autographs With Prices*.

Burdick, Loraine
5 Court Place
Puyallup, WA 98372
Semi-monthly list of movie memorabilia for 75 cents. Clippings also sold.

Classic Images
P. O. Box 809
Muscatine, IA 52761
$25 per year for monthly tabloid devoted to classic film.

Collectors' United
P. O. Box 1160
Chatsworth, GA 30705
$20 per year for monthly publication of classified ads for buying and selling dolls and related items.

Doll Reader
Hobby House Press
900 Frederick Street
Cumberland, MD 21502
$24.00 per year for eight issues. Information on both antique and modern dolls.

Frasher's Doll Auctions, Inc.
Rt 1-Box 142
Oak Grove, MO 64075
$25 for doll auction catalogues. Mail order bids accepted.

Hake's Americana and Collectibles
P. O. Box 1444
York, PA 17405
$20 for four catalogues. Mail and phone bid auction specializing in character and personality collectibles.

Luton's Theater Poster Exchange
2780 Frayser Blvd.
P. O. Box 27621
Memphis, TN 38127
$3.00 for catalogue of vintage posters.

National Assoc. of Fan Clubs
P. O. Box 4559
Pueblo, CO 81003
$12.00 per year for four newsletters. $8.00 for Fan Club Directory

Paper Collector's Marketplace
P. O. Box 127
Scandinavia, WI 54977
$15.95 per year for twelve issues. Classified ads and articles.

Searle's Autographs
P. O. Box 849
Woodbine, Georgia 31569
Catalogs of autographs for sale $5.00 per year

Sy Sussman
2962 S. Mann St.
Las Vegas, Nevada 89102
8" by 10" glossy pictures of thousands of stars $1.00 each

Bibliography

Astaire, Fred. *Steps in Time*. New York: Harper and Brothers, 1959.

Axe, John. *The Collectible Dionne Quintuplets*. Riverdale, Maryland (now in Cumberland, Maryland): Hobby House Press, 1977.

Axe, John. *Collectible Sonja Henie*. Cumberland, Maryland: Hobby House Press, 1979.

Axe, John. *Encyclopedia of Celebrity Dolls*. Cumberland, Maryland: Hobby House Press, 1983.

Bergen, Candice. *Knock Wood*. New York: Simon and Schuster, 1984.

Berton, Pierce. *The Dionne Years*. New York: W.W. Norton Co., 1977.

Black, Shirley Temple. *Child Star*. New York: McGraw-Hill Publishing Co., 1988.

Bodeen, Dewitt. *More From Hollywood: The Careers of 15 Great American Stars*. New York: A. S. Barnes and Co., 1977.

Block, Maxine, ed. "Chaplin, Charlie", "Jolson, Al." *Current Biography 1940*. New York: H. W. Wilson Co., 1940.

Block, Maxine, ed. "Deanna Durbin", *Current Biography 1941*. New York: H. W. Wilson Co., 1941.

Blum, Daniel and Revised by John Kobal. *A New Pictorial History of the Talkies*. New York: Perigee Books (G. P. Putnam's Sons), 1982.

Bookbinder, Robert. *The Films of Bing Crosby*. Secaucus, New Jersey: Citadel Press, 1977.

Brough, James with Annette, Cecile, Marie and Yvonne Dionne. *We Were Five*. New York: Simon and Schuster, 1965.

Burdick, Loraine. *The Shirley Temple Scrapbook*. Middle Village, New York: Jonathan David Publishers, 1975.

Cagney, James. *Cagney by Cagney*. Garden City, New York: Doubleday and Co., 1976.

Carpozi, George. *The Fabulous Life of Bing Crosby*. New York: Manor Books, Inc., 1977.

Carpozi, George. *The John Wayne Story*. New York: Dell Publishing Co., 1974.

Chaneles, Sol. *Collecting Movie Memorabilia*. New York: Arco Publishing Co., 1977.

Crosby, Bing (as told to Pete Martin). *Call Me Lucky*. New York: Simon and Schuster, 1953.

Crosby, Gary and Ross Firestone. *Going My Own Way*. Garden City, New York: Doubleday and Co., 1983.

Crowther, Bosley. *Vintage Films*. New York: G. P.Putnam's Sons, 1977.

Croy, Homer. *Our Will Rogers*. New York: Duell, Sloan and Pearce, 1953.

Deans, Mickey and Ann Pinchot. *Weep No More My Lady* (Judy Garland). New York: Pyramid Books,1973.

Eames, John Douglas. *The MGM Story*. New York: Crown Publishers, 1976.

Edelson, Edward. *Great Kids of the Movies*. Garden City, N. Y.: Doubleday and Co., 1979.

Edwards, Anne. *Judy Garland*. New York: Simon and Schuster, 1975.

Finch, Christopher. *Rainbow: The Stormy Life of Judy Garland*. New York: Grosset and Dunlap, 1975.

Fisher, John. *Call Them Irreplaceable*. New York: Stein and Day, 1974.

Fitzgerald, Michael G. *Universal Pictures*. New York: Arlington House Pub., 1977.

Foulke, Jan. *9th Blue Book Dolls and Values*. Cumberland, Maryland: Hobby House Press, 1989.

Franklin, Joe. *Classics of the Silent Screen*. Secaucus, New Jersey: The Citadel Press, 1973.

Goldstein, Norm/The Associated Press. *John Wayne: A Tribute*. New York: Holt, Rinehart and Winston, 1979.

Hanna, David. *The Life and times of John Wayne*. Lorelei Pub. Co., 1979.

Harris, Warren G. *Gable and Lombard*. New York: Simon and Schuster, 1974.

Henie, Sonja. *Wings on my Feet*. New York: Prentice Hall, 1945.

Huff, Theodore. *Charlie Chaplin*. New York: Pyramid Books, 1972.

Jewell, Richard B. with Vernon Harbin. *The RKO Story*. New York: Crown Publishers, 1982.

Keylin, Arleen and Suri Fleischer, ed. *Hollywood Album Lives and Deaths of Hollywood Stars from the Pages of The New York Times*. New York: Arno Press, 1979.

Keylin, Arleen, ed. *Hollywood Album 2: Lives and Deaths of Hollywood Stars from the Pages of the New York Times*. New York: Arno Press, 1979.

Kobal, John. *Rita Hayworth; Portrait of a Love Goddess*. New York: W. W. Norton, 1978.

Lloyd, Ann and Graham, Fuller, ed. *The Illustrated Who's Who of the Cinema*. New York: Portland House, 1987.

Longest, David. *Character Toys and Collectibles Second Series*. Paducah, KY: Collector Books, 1987.

Maltin, Leonard, ed. *Leonard Maltin's TV Movies 1985-1986 edition*. New York: New American Library, 1984.

Michael, Paul. *The Academy Awards*. New York: Crown Publishers, Inc., 1978.

Michael, Paul. *The Great American Movie Book*. Englewood Cliffs, New Jersey: Prentice-Hall Inc. 1980.

Mordden, Ethan. *The Hollywood Musical*. New York: St. Martin's Press, 1981.

Morella, Joe and Edward Z. Epstein. *Gable and Lombard and Powell and Harlow*. New York: Dell Publishing, 1975.

Morella, Joe and Edward Z. Epstein. *Judy; The Films and Career of Judy Garland*. London: Leslie Frewin, 1969.

Morella, Joe and Edward Z. Epstein. *Rita: The Life of Rita Hayworth*. New York: Delacorte Press, 1983.

Morella, Joe, Edward Z. Epstein and John Griggs. *The Films of World War II*. Secaucus, New Jersey. The Citadel Press, 1980.

O'Brien, P. J. *Will Rogers: Ambassador of Good Will*. 1935.

Peary, Danny. *Close-Ups: The Movie Star Book*. New York: Workman Publishing Co., 1978.

Ragan, David. *Who's Who in Hollywood 1900-1976*. New Rochelle, New York: Arlington House Pub., 1976.

Ramer, Jean. *Duke: The Real Story of John Wayne*. New York: Charter Books, 1979.

Ringgold, Gene. *The Films of Rita Hayworth*. Secaucus, New Jersey: Citadel Press, 1974.

Rothe, Anna, ed. "Astaire, Fred", Bergen, Edgar." *Current Biography*. New York: H. W. Wilson Co., 1945.

Scherman, David E., ed. *Life Goes to the Movies*. New York: Time-Life Books, 1975.

Schickel, Richard. *The Stars*. New York: Bonanza Books, 1962.

Sennett, Ted. *Warner Brothers Presents*. Secaucus, N. J.: Castle Books (Book Sales, Inc.), 1971.

Shepherd, Donald; and Robert E. Slatzer. *Bing Crosby: The Hollow Man*. New York: St. Martin's Press, 1981.

Shipman, David. *The Great Movie Stars*. New York: Bonanza Books, 1970.

Silke, James R. *Here's Looking At You Kid: 50 Years of Fighting, Working and Dreaming at Warner Bros.*. Boston: Little, Brown and Co., 1976.

Slide, Anthony. *A Collectors Guide to Movie Memorabilia With Prices*. Des Moines, Iowa (now in Radnor, PA): Wallace-Homestead, 1983.

Smith, Patricia. *Doll Values: Antique to Modern Series Six*. Paducah, KY: Collector Books, 1990.

Smith, Patricia R. *Shirley Temple Dolls and Collectibles*. Paducah, KY: Collector Books, 1977.

Smith, Patricia R. *Shirley Temple Doll and Collectibles: Second Series*. Paducah, KY: Collector Books, 1979.

Springer, John. *All Talking! All Singing! All Dancing! A Pictorial History of the Movie Musical*. New York: Cadillac Pub. Co., 1966.

Sterling, Bryan, ed. *The Will Rogers Scrapbook*. New York: Bonanza Books, 1976.

Stuart, Ray. *Immortals of the Screen*. New York: Bonanza Books, 1965.

Thomas, Bob. *The One and Only Bing*. New York: Ace Books, 1977.

Tornabene, Lyn. *Long Live the King: Biography of Clark Gable*. New York: G.P. Putnam's Sons, 1976.

Wlaschin, Ken. *The Illustrated Encyclopedia of the World's Great Movie Stars and Their Films*. New York: Harmony Books, 1979.

Woodcock, Jean. *Paper Dolls of Famous Faces*. Binghamton, New York: Printed by Niles and Phippe, 1974.

Young, Mary. *A Collector's Guide to Paper Dolls*. Paducah, Kentucky: Collector Books, 1980.

Zinman, David. *50 Classic Motion Pictures*. New York: Bonanza Books, 1970

Value Guide

The prices in this value guide should only be used as a guide and should not be used to set prices for movie memorabilia. Prices vary from one section of the country to another and also from dealer to dealer. The prices listed are the best estimates the author can give at the time of publication, but prices in the collectible field can change quickly. Neither the author nor the publisher assumes responsibility for any losses that might be incurred as a result of consulting this guide.

Prices listed for dolls vary greatly because the condition of the doll, its original clothing, tags, box, etc. make a difference in the cost of a collectible doll. The paper doll prices are listed for cut or uncut material according to the way the paper dolls are pictured. Generally uncut books cost three to four times more than cut paper dolls. If an item pictured is an ad from a magazine, the price listed is for the tear sheet alone. If an item is an article or a cover from a magazine, the price listed is for the entire publication.

Items that are torn or very worn or have missing parts would be priced less than the prices listed in this guide and items that are mint with tags, boxes, etc. would be priced higher than the prices listed.

Page	Position	Price Range
5	TL	$65-75
6	TL	$35-45
6	TR	$5-8
6	BR	$10-12
7	TL	$10-12
7	TR	$10-12
7	BL	$10-12
7	BR	$10-12
8	TL	$15-20
8	BL	$10-12
8	BR	$120-150
9	TL	$8-10
9	TR	$5-10
9	BL	$40-50
10	TL	$15-20
10	TR	$15-20
10	BL	$85-100
11	TL	$3-5
11	CR	$8-10
11	BL	$3-5
12	TL	$15-20
12	BL	$3-5
12	BR	$5-8
13	TL	$3-5
13	BL	$40-50
13	CR	$15-20
14	TL	$5-8
14	TR	$20-25
14	BL	$35-45
15	CR	$75-85
16	TL	$3-6
17	TL	$25-35
17	TR	$3-5
17	BR	$3-5
18	TL	$8-10
18	BL	$2-4
18	CR	$10-15
19	TL	$2-4
19	TR	$3-5
19	BR	$5-8
20	TR	$20-25
20	BL	$8-10 each
21	TL	$2-4
21	TR	$35-45
21	TL	$5-8
21	BR	$20-30
22	TL	$35-45
22	CR	$75-85
22	BR	$60-75
23	TL	$10-15
24	TL	$35-45
25	TL	$350-450
25	TR	$35-45
26	TL	$300-500 (doll)
26	TL	$20-25 (pencil box)
26	TR	$25-35
26	BR	$600 and up
27	TL	$50-60
27	BL	$20-25
27	BR	$15-20
28	TL	$100-125
28	BL	$8-10
29	TL	$35-45
29	CR	$12-15
29	BL	$35-50
30	TL	$15-20
30	TR	$30-40
30	BL	$5-8
30	BR	$10-15 each
31	TL	$250-300
31	BL	$15-18
32	TR	$45-55
32	BL	$10-15
33	TL	$10-15
34	TR	$5-8
34	BL	$5-8
34	BR	$10-15
35	TL	$10-15
35	BL	$5-8
35	BR	$10-15
36	TL	$5-8
36	TR	$2-4
36	BL	$2-4
36	BR	$15-20
37	TR	$10-15
37	BL	$2-4
37	BR	$5-8
38	TL	$2-4
38	TR	$5-8
38	BR	$20-25
39	TL	$5-8
39	TR	$25-35
40	TL	$35-50
40	CR	$50-65
40	BL	$30-40
41	TL	Dolls: 7" $100-125
41	TL	10" $150-250
41	TL	20" $200-500
41	TL	Book $25-35
41	TR	$15-20
42	TL	$5-8
42	BR	$5-10
43	TL	$20-30
43	BR	$3-5
44	TL	$3-5
44	TR	$125-150
44	BR	$900-1200 set
45	TL	$1000-1500 set
45	BL	$175-400
46	TR	$40-50
46	BL	$175-225
47	TL	$50-75
47	CL	$40-50
47	CR	$100-125
47	BL	$ 50-75
48	TL	$40-50 (part of set)
48	TR	$15-20
48	BL	$15-20
48	BR	$15-20
49	TL	$15-20
49	TR	$10-12
49	BL	$25-35
49	BR	$10-12
50	TL	$50-60
50	TR	$65-75 (full deck)
50	CR	$5-10
50	BL	$35-45
51	TL	$5-10
51	TR	$5-10
51	CL	$5-10
51	CR	$5-10
51	BL	$5-10
51	BR	$5-10
52	TL	$3-5
52	TR	$3-5
52	BL	$3-5
52	BR	$2-4
53	TL	$3-5
53	TR	$3-5
53	BL	$3-5
53	BC	$3-5
53	BR	$3-5
54	TR	$20-30
54	BL	$100-125 set
55	TL	$5-10
55	TR	$10-15
55	BL	Display $100 & up
55	BL	Dolls 8" set $900 & up
55	BL	14" $150-350
56	TR	$8-10
56	BL	$15-18
57	TL	$15-18
57	BL	$15-18
58	TL	$15-20 each
58	CR	$25-30
58	BR	$20-25
59	TL	$20-25
59	CR	$20-25
59	BR	$20-25
60	TL	$20-25
60	BL	$10-15
60	BR	$20-25
61	TL	$20-25
61	CL	$20-25
61	BL	$20-25
62	TL	$20-25
62	TR	$20-25
62	BL	$20-25
62	BR	$20-25
63	TL	$20-25
63	BL	$20-25
63	TR	$20-25
63	BR	$20-25
64	TL	$20-25
64	CR	$25-30
64	BL	$20-25
65	TL	$12-15
65	TR	$12-15
65	BL	$12-15
65	BR	$12-15
66	TL	$5-8
66	CL	$25-30
66	CR	$25-35
66	BL	$25-35
66	BR	$25-35
67	TL	$25-30
67	TR	$25-35
67	CL	$25-35
67	CR	$15-20
67	BL	$25-35
68	TL	$30-35
68	TR	$15-20
68	BL	$30-35
68	BR	$15-20
69	TR	$12-15
69	BL	$12-15
70	BL	$5-8
70	BR	$15-20
71	TL	$15-20
71	BR	$10-12
72	TL	$8-10
72	BR	$8-10
73	TR	$300-600
73	BL	$200-400
74	TR	$45-65
74	CL	$125-175
74	BR	$10-12
75	TL	$30-40
75	TR	$10-15
75	BL	$30-40
75	BR	$18-22
76	TL	$5-8
76	TR	$5-8
76	BL	$40-60
77	TR	$12-15
77	BL	$15-18
77	BR	$5-8
78	TL	$12-15
78	TR	$5-8
78	BL	$5-8
79	TR	$5-8
79	CL	$5-8
79	BR	$25-35
80	TL	$15-20
81	TL	$15-20
81	TR	$5-8
81	BL	$20-30
82	TL	$10-12
82	TR	$75-125
82	BL	$5-8
83	TL	$8-10
83	TR	$25-30
83	BL	$25-30
84	TR	$40-50
84	BR	$3-5
84	BL	$75-85
85	TL	$3-5
85	TR	$15-20
85	BL	$5-8
85	BR	$12-15
86	TL	$10-12
86	TR	$35-45
86	BR	$30-40
87	TL	$15-20
87	BL	$35-50
87	BR	$5-8
88	TL	$15-20
89	TR	$8-10
89	BL	$500-900
89	BR	$3-5
90	TL	$3-5
90	TR	$2-4
90	BL	$10-12
91	TL	$20-25
91	TR	$10-15
91	BL	$15-20
91	BR	$75-100
92	TL	$35-50
92	TR	$8-10
93	TL	$45-55
93	BL	$45-65
93	BR	$35-50
94	TL	$12-15
94	TR	$8-10
94	BL	$12-15
94	BR	$2-4
95	TL	$10-12
95	BR	$2-4
95	BL	$8-10
96	TL	$15-20
96	TR	$10-12
96	BL	$40-50
97	TL	$25-30
97	BL	$8-10
97	BR	$50 & up
98	BR	$65-85
99	TL	$12-15
100	BL	$5-8
100	TR	$5-8
100	TR	$5-8
101	TL	$3-5
101	TR	$5-8
101	BL	$5-8
102	TL	$40-60
102	TR	$40 -50
102	BL	$150-200
102	BR	$10-12
103	TL	$30-40

No.	Loc	Price
103	TR	$8-10
103	BL	$30-40
104	TL	$2-4
104	TR	$5-8
104	BL	$5-8
104	BR	$20-25
105	TL	$2-4
105	TR	$15-20
105	BR	$20-25
106	BL	$12-15
106	LR	$75-100
107	TL	$15-20
108	TR	$3-5
108	BL	$15-18
108	BR	$100-125
109	TL	$2 4
109	TR	$40-50
109	BL	$45-65
110	TR	$12-15
110	BL	$5-8
110	BR	$12-15
111	TL	$2-4
111	TR	$2-4
111	BL	$3-5
112	TL	$100-125
112	TR	$25-35
112	BL	$175-275
112	BR	$12-18
113	TL	$15-20
113	TR	$35-50
113	DR	$30 40
114	TR	$100-125
114	BL	$8-12
114	BR	$5-8
115	TL	$5-8
116	TR	$3-5
116	BL	$3-5
116	BR	$8-10
117	TL	$8-10
117	TR	$15-20
117	BL	$15-20
118	BL	$200-400
118	TR	$175-200
118	BR	$35-50
119	TL	$5-8
119	TR	$75-85
119	CR	$40-60
119	BL	$12-15
119	BR	$20-25
120	TL	$165-185
120	TR	$5-8
120	BR	$12-15
121	TL	$15-18
121	TR	$2-4
121	BL	$35-45
122	TL	$3-5
122	BR	$5-8
123	BL	$15-20
123	CR	$85-150
124	TL	$95-200
124	TR	Pin $25-30
124	BL	$150-300
124	BR	$10-15
125	TR	$15-20
125	BL	$15-20
125	BR	$35-40
126	TL	$40-50
126	TR	$8-10
126	CR	$22-28
126	BR	$5-10
127	TL	$75-100
128	TL	$8-10
128	TR	$8-10
128	BL	$8-10
128	BR	$3-5
129	TL	$10-12
129	TR	$20-30
129	BR	$5-8
130	TL	$35-50
130	TR	$25-35
130	BR	$5-8
131	TL	$15-18
131	BL	$20-25
131	BR	$15-20
132	TL	$8-12

No.	Loc	Price
132	CR	$10-15
132	BL	$5-8
133	TR	$5-8
133	CL	$5-8
133	BR	$8-10
134	TL	$5-8
134	BR	$8-10
135	TR	$15-20
135	BL	$8-10
135	BR	$8-10
136	TL	$8-10
136	TR	$3-5
136	BR	$8-10
137	TL	$5-8
137	TR	$8-10
137	BL	$3-5
137	BR	$15-18
138	TL	$15-20
138	TR	$5-8
138	BR	$20-25
139	TL	$200 & up
139	TR	$3-5
139	BL	$50-75
140	TL	$12-15
140	BL	$75-85
140	BR	$65-75
141	TL	$45-55
141	CR	$10-15
141	BR	$25 35
142	TL	$250-350
143	TL	$8-15
143	BR	$40-55
144	TL	$12-15
144	TR	$85-110
144	BL	$3-5
145	TL	$30-40
145	TR	Radio $350 & up
145	BL	$200-275
145	BR	$20-25
146	TL	$25-30
146	TR	$15-20
146	BL	$40-75
146	BR	$45-60
147	TL	$30-40
147	TR	$30-40
147	BL	$35-50
148	TR	$12-18
148	BL	$20-25
148	BR	Magazine $3-5
148	BR	Spoon $15-20
149	TL	$15-20
149	BL	$18-22
149	TR	$25-35
150	TL	$25-35
150	TR	$10-12
151	TL	$3-5
151	TR	$15-20
151	BL	$3-5
152	TL	Wind-up $200-250
152	TL	Doll $150-225
152	BR	$60-75
153	TL	$8-10
154	TL	$2-4
154	BL	$12-15
154	BR	$3-5
155	TL	$12-15
155	TR	$275-600
155	BL	$2-4
156	TL	$175-200
156	TR	$30-45
156	BL	$40-50
156	BR	$8-10
157	TR	$15-20
157	BL	$12-15
157	BR	$18-22
158	TL	$20-25
158	TR	$8-12
158	BL	$8-10
158	BR	$20-25
159	TL	$35-45
159	TR	$20-25
159	BL	$15-20
160	TR	$5-8
160	BL	$15-20
161	TL	$4-8

No.	Loc	Price
162	TR	$5-8
162	BR	$4-6
163	TR	$3-5
163	BL	$3-5
163	BR	$25-30
164	TL	$15-18
164	BL	$25-35
165	TL	$15-20
165	TR	$15-20
165	BR	$12-15
166	TL	$15-20
166	TR	$10-15
166	BL	$35-45
167	TL	$20-25
167	TR	$75-100
167	BL	$5-8
167	BR	$8-10
168	TL	$20-25
168	BR	$20-30
169	TL	Dolls: 29" $600-1000
169	TL	15" $300-600
169	TL	12" vinyl 75-150
169	TL	Books $20-30
169	TL	Sheet Music $15-20
170	TR	$3-5
170	BL	$15-20
170	BR	$10-15
171	TL	$15-20
171	TR	$5-8
171	BL	$50 & up
172	TL	$50 & up
172	TR	$400-700
172	BL	$40-60
172	BR	$50 & up
173	TL	$300-600
173	TR	$500-900
174	TL	$50-65
174	BL	$50-75
174	BR	$100-125
175	TL	$50-75
175	TR	$50-75
175	BL	$50-75
176	TL	$35-50
176	TR	$35-50
176	BL	$35-50
177	TR	$18-25
177	BL	$3-5
177	BR	$15-20
178	TL	$25-30
178	TR	$25-30
178	BL	$25-30
178	BR	$15-20
179	TL	$25-35
179	BL	$15-20
179	BR	$20-30
180	TL	$20-30
180	TR	$20-25 (empty)
180	BL	$20-25
180	BR	$20-25
181	TL	$25-35
181	TR	$25-35
181	BL	$25-35
181	BR	$25-35
182	TL	$35-45
182	BL	$15-20
183	TL	$25-30
183	TR	$20-30
183	BL	$35-55
184	TL	$15-20
184	TR	$125-250
184	BL	$15-20
184	BR	Buggy $275 & up
185	TL	$4-6
185	TR	$30-35
185	BL	$8-15
185	BR	$25-35
186	TL	$25-35
186	TR	$35-50
186	BL	$5-6
187	TL	$15-20
187	TR	$25-30
187	BL	$3-5
188	TR	$25-35
188	BL	$30-35
189	TL	$35-45

No.	Loc	Price
189	TR	$5 8
189	BL	$25-30
189	BR	$100-125
190	TL	$15-20
190	TR	$5-8
190	BL	Sheet music $15-20
190	BL	Program $20-25
191	TL	$12-15
191	DL	$10 15
192	TL	$35-40
192	TR	$3-5
192	BL	$10-15
193	TL	$15-20
193	TR	$15-20
193	BL	$20-25
193	BR	$15-20
194	TL	$30-35
194	TR	$20-25
194	BL	$20-25
194	BR	$10-12
195	TL	$15-18
195	BR	Tagged doll $125
195	BR	Other $85
196	TL	Catalog $40-45
196	BL	$20-25
196	BR	$50-60
197	TL	$50-60
197	TR	$25-35
197	BL	$40-60
197	BR	$25-35
198	TL	$15-18 each
198	BL	$15-20
198	BR	$15-20
199	TR	$30-40
199	BR	$12-15 each
200	TL	$50-125
200	TR	$10-15
200	BR	$8-12
201	TL	$25-40
201	BL	$10-15
201	BR	$40-50
202	TL	$8-10
203	TL	$4-6
203	TR	$2-4
203	BR	$8-10
204	TR	$2-4
204	BL	$2-4
204	BR	$2-4
205	TR	$3-5
205	BR	$4-6
206	TR	$25-30
206	BR	$20-25
207	TL	$20-25
207	TR	$8-12
207	BL	$35-40
208	TL	$15-20
208	TR	$15-18
208	BL	$15-25
208	BR	$10-15
209	BL	$35-45
209	BR	$8-12
210	TL	$75-85
210	BR	$35-45
211	TL	$5-8
212	TL	$35-45
212	BL	$20-25
212	BR	$5-10 each
213	TL	$300-800
213	BR	$25-35
214	TL	$90-100
214	TR	$5-8
214	BL	$15-20
214	BR	$5-8
215	TR	$35-45
215	BL	$50-60
215	BR	$15-18
216	TL	$55-75
216	TR	$10-12
216	BR	$150-175
217	TR	$15-20
217	BL	$20-25
217	BR	$20-25
218	TR	$15-20
218	BL	$12-15
218	BR	$2-4

About the Author

Dian Zillner is an avid collector of movie memorabilia. She has been a frequent contributor to *The Antique Trader* and *Doll Reader* with many articles published on dolls, paper dolls, and movie collectibles.

She holds a Bachelor's Degree from Pittsburg State University (Kansas) and a Master's from Northwest Missouri State University and is currently the high school librarian in Maryville, Missouri.

Dian Zillner is presently working on several projects including a book on dolls for beginning collectors.